I dedicate this small book to my children,
the bravest people I know —
and to the memory of their father, who gave them to me.

FIGURING SH!T OUT

LOVE, LAUGHTER, SUICIDE, AND SURVIVAL

AMY BIANCOLLI

Behler
PUBLICATIONS
USA

Behler Publications

Figuring Sh!t Out
A Behler Publications Book

Copyright © 2015 by Amy Biancolli
Cover design by Yvonne Parks - www.pearcreative.ca.
Back cover photography by Danny Richardson
Interior photography by "Dad II"

Library of Congress Cataloging-in-Publication Data

Biancolli, Amy.
  Figuring shit out : love, laughter, suicide, and survival : a memoir / by Amy Biancolli.
      pages cm
  ISBN-13: 978-1-933016-52-8 (pbk.)
  ISBN-10: 1-933016-52-3 (pbk.)
  1. Biancolli, Amy. 2. Biancolli, Amy--Family. 3. Journalists--United States--
Biography. 4. Film critics--United States--Biography. I. Title.
  PN4874.B465A3 2014
  818'.603--dc23
  [B]

                          2014016264

FIRST PRINTING ·

ISBN 13: 978-1-933016-52-8
e-book ISBN 978-1-933016-46-7

Published by Behler Publications, LLC
USA
www.behlerpublications.com

Manufactured in the United States of America

Table of Contents

1. Cops, *1*
2. Things I Can't Say to Your Face, Part I, *5*
3. Social Security, *10*
4. Improvisation, *13*
5. The Hall Pass, *15*
6. What I Do When I Do What I Do, *19*
7. The Casserole Club Has Now Come to Order, *21*
8. Two, Two, Two People at Once, *25*
9. And Now, a Few Words about Guilt, *27*
10. Holy Shit, *29*
11. In Which I Begin to Resemble Alaskan Wildlife, *32*
12. The Things I'm Not, *36*
13. The Lasts, *40*
14. F.S.O., Part I, *43*
15. Lost in Space, *46*
16. Thanksgiving, *48*
17. Not a Sad Tink, *53*
18. Smaller, *58*
19. Things I Can't Say to Your Face, Part II, *60*
20. In Which I Begin to Regard My Legs Anew, *64*
21. The Checkout Line Jollies, Part I, *67*
22. We Three Rings, *70*
23. Looking for Mr. Manly Pants, Part I, *75*
24. F.S.O., Part II, *78*
25. Stink and Weeds, *81*
26. Ecuador Stories, Part I: Arrival, *84*
27. Ecuador Stories, Part II: The Middle, *89*
28. Ecuador Stories, Part III: Whitewater, *92*
29. Ecuador Stories, Part IV: Shit, *96*
30. Ecuador Stories, Part V: Monkeys, More Monkeys, and a Dog, *101*
31. I Really Need To Say This Out Loud, *108*
32. The Hitchhiker, *111*
33. Things I Can't Say To Your Face, Part III, *118*
34. Alone with Electra, *124*
35. New Amy Loads the Dishwasher, *129*
36. W.G.W., *134*
37. Memo to Clooney Redux, *140*
38. The Checkout Line Jollies, Part II, *144*
39. At Rainbow Narrows, *149*

40. Looking for Mr. Manly Pants, Part II, *154*
41. Things I Can't Say to Your Face, Part IV, *160*
42. My Homie, Job, *165*
43. Unemployment, *171*
44. The Wisdom of the Pam, *176*
45. Things I Can't Say to Your Face, Part V, *179*
46. Oh My God, *182*
47. The Checkout Line Jollies, Part III, *184*
48. Belaying and Belayed, *187*
49. Isabella, *190*
50. Snails, *192*

Chris Ringwald Bio, *197*
Acknowledgments, *199*

1 Cops

"Your life isn't over."

My dad says this. He's in my kitchen, sitting on one of those 1950s metal-tube chairs, tapping his forefinger on the table. "Do you hear me? It's not over."

I know, I assure him. I have the kids. They need me. They're my life now.

"No," he says. "I mean, YOUR life isn't over. Beyond the kids. You'll go on living, doing things. This isn't it."

I know that, I say.

"OK," he replies, then grunts—more of a brief hum. He only hums when he thinks I'm full of shit.

No, really. Really, I say. You're right. My life isn't over. I know that. I know that. So stop tapping your finger. BECAUSE I KNOW THAT.

Do I know that? How the hell can I possibly know that? Only a few hours earlier, Chris, my beloved husband of twenty years, jumped to his death off the roof of a parking garage a mile from our home. Cops came to the house in a pair to tell me, just like in the movies. Ding-dong, your husband's dead. Your life is over. Except it's not.

So my dad sits in the kitchen, bucking me up. He arrived an hour earlier, after I'd already broken the news to my two younger kids. My 15-year-old, Jeanne, was home sick and, seeing the police, collapsed on the staircase in tears. I fell around her, into her sobs, saying nothing and everything at once. Then I pulled 11-year-old Mitchell from school and told him and held him on the broad lawn outside, unsure if even holding him could help. Later tonight I'll have to tell Madeleine, my 17-year-old, on a gap year in Ecuador. That will be a monstrous phone call. I dread it.

These are the hardest things I've ever done, ever will do, could ever imagine doing. Think of the difficult tasks in your past: climbing a mountain, writing a book, squeezing out a human being into the bright chaos of living. Telling children that their dad committed suicide—that yes, he loved them, yes, they'll get through this, and no, it wasn't their fault—is incomprehensibly harder. As though you would even try to comprehend such a thing until it happens to you. You wouldn't. There's no point. Stop trying.

Neighbors and friends are tracking in and out. Charitable souls have mowed the lawn. Hauled out the garbage. Cleared out the fridge. Organized the influx of food. A sign-up sheet for meals sits on the porch. Soon we'll have dinner covered through November, and it's now September 26. Someone, at some point, hands me a sandwich. Later, I'll be calling Madeleine to say the worst and tell her to pack for her flight home. Tomorrow, my dad and I will visit the funeral home. The day after tomorrow: the wake. The day after the day after tomorrow: the funeral. The day after the day after the day after the day after the day after the day after tomorrow: My husband will still be dead.

My life isn't over. My dad is right. I'm only 48; there's still some juice in the old girl. Still breathing for the time being. But what life will it be without my promised mate? Twenty years ago, we vowed to stick it out together, and stick it out we did—knowing one of us would leave first. Just not so soon. Not this way. And dammit, not with cops.

Dad comes with me to the funeral home, along with my friend Alicia. We're brought to a small, bland, windowless room where we discuss wake details and pall bearers and church fees and cremation. I've done this all a few times before, so I know what to say. And the most important thing to say is: I AM BUYING A JAR.

Saying this is imperative because, otherwise, the funeral home will try to sell you a $300 plastic urn—and, let's face it, an urn is just a vase with a sealed top. A jar. Which you can buy for thirty or forty bucks or so at any home-decor shop at any strip mall in any suburb anywhere. When my mother died, my friend Tamar and I bought a lovely floral vase at the Pier One Imports on Wolf Road in Colonie, west of Albany. We buried Mama's ashes just fine in that thing. Capped it and kissed it, and down it went.

And so at the funeral home I declare my intentions thusly: I AM BUYING A JAR.

"You can do that."

Funeral directors love to say this: "You can do that," as though, excuse me, I can't do whatever the shizz I want.

We discuss other things. Photos and music for the memorial video. The priest for the funeral. The cemetery. I study this man doing the talking, a sleek late 30s model in a dark suit, and the quiet fellow sitting beside him, a kind, gray undertaker, who came as part of the package when two funeral homes merged last year.

The sleek one asks about caskets for the wake and funeral Mass. I say I'd like to rent one. "You can do that," he says. Then he goes on to explain that some people prefer not to put their loved ones into a coffin that's been previously occupied. Oh, I say. Not me. It makes no difference to me how many other corpses have lain in the thing. Me, I'd like to rent one. And he says, again: "You can do that." So affirming! And such shiny hair! I wonder idly about his product.

Still, I am forced to go on a tour of the casket room. I am not sure why I am forced to go on a tour of the casket room, and the little gray undertaker doesn't seem sure, either. He is almost apologetic as he takes me straight to the lone rental option. Oh, I say. That's nice. I'll take that one. Then he guides me over to a strange, molded plastic container with rounded corners and a lid. It is roughly the size and shape of a picnic cooler. It costs several hundred dollars. The kind, gray undertaker explains its purpose: to hold the urn—that is, the jar that I plan on buying.

You mean, it's an urn for the urn, I say.

"Yes," says the little gray man.

Ummm, and why would I need an urn for the urn?

"You wouldn't," he says, and for the first time in my life I want to French-kiss an undertaker.

I had always thought one urn was enough. I had always thought the whole point of cremation was reduce, reuse, recycle. Apparently not. Apparently it is just an excuse for yet more packaging. I don't plan on paying any more visits to funeral homes any time soon, but if I did, I would expect to be marched into a casket room lined with rows and rows of urns sized from small to large, like Russian nesting dolls. An urn within an urn within an urn, an infinite progression of crockery to impress the newly bereaved.

Later, with girlfriends so close I call them sisters—Pam, Jane, Tamar, and Sue—I visit that same Pier One and choose a jar for Chris's ashes. Recalling his green thumb, we select a cookie jar splashed with bright yellow flowers and a nice, knobby, nippled top. For $36 plus change. Perfecto.

In the parking lot, we laugh and hug and go our separate ways, and I head home with the jar on the floor behind me. Already, I've lived two days my husband didn't, laughed at jokes he never heard, made decisions without his input. This makes no sense. It never will. And yet, I know to my core, with the irrational cellular conviction of a living organism at loose in the world, that I can and will and must propel inexorably forward.

2 Things I Can't Say to Your Face, Part I

I wish I could see you. I wish I could feel you, smell you, taste you, throw my arms around you, accidentally step on your feet, press my head against your chest, run my tongue along your lips, and slap you playfully on the ass. I wish I could make love to you. The fact that I can't sucks, although not literally, because if it did, we'd both be getting a little action right now.

I thought you were hot the first time I saw you. Remember that? At a picnic of young journalists at Look Park in lovely Northampton, Massachusetts. You were smiling, sturdy, strong. I checked out your legs. In the middle of the picnic you decided to go for a run—training for a marathon—and when you returned, you were a fine and sweaty masculine beast. Again, I checked out your legs. I observed the band of fat around your waist, a permanent feature that never had anything to do with how much or how little you exercised, and I decided it didn't bother me. Your hands were square, your biceps were thick, your forearms exploded like Popeye's. Your eyes, maybe light blue, maybe gray—I could never decide which—sparked with joy and humor as we spoke.

You talked about a series you were writing for the Albany *Times Union*. New York's Iroquois, you told me. You had traveled to settlements all over the state. No kidding! I said. How interesting! I said. Tell me about it! I said, continuing to check out the hotness of your arms and legs. I had no idea you were checking me out, too. Later, the young journalists moved their partying to a friend's house nearby, and there I positioned myself on a couch between you and an ex of mine. A nice ex, only briefly dated—for a week, maybe? Jim. I know you remember him.

You and I talked more. About books and music this time. We discovered we both loved opera. Matt, a mutual friend, was complaining about some guy he knew whose "personality changed" when he fell in love and married. Matt was grumbling about the negative effects of dating. You turned to me and asked, "Do *you* negatively affect the personalities of the men you date?" And I turned to Jim and asked, Gee, I don't know, Jim— do I? And Jim, caught off guard, spat out a sequence of unrelated and unintelligible noises that translated, roughly, as "I have no idea, and *please* leave me out of it if you two are planning to flirt."

Which we did, yessirree. When I got up to leave for the drive back to Boston, you took my phone number. Told me you'd call. Which you did, yessirree. Took me to hear Harry Connick. Drove to Boston to attend Mass with me (our second date! What good Catholics!). Cooked me a stir-fry in Albany, held hands with me, kissed me wildly across the same metal kitchen table where I grieved with my dad a lifetime later. Fell breathless to your knees and kissed me some more. So much kissing. Hours that became decades of kissing, kissing, kissing. Strange that it's all past. Strange that I can't kiss you now—only your photographs, which I smooch when no one's looking.

How I long to touch you. How I long to see your smile, smell your musk, hear your heavy footsteps on the stairs.

You were the man of my dreams. The answer to my prayers. You were the one I didn't know I needed when I wrote up my list of attributes—everything I desired in a man—and sent it up as a prayer to God. This hypothetical manly-man had to love God. He had to love me. He had to be faithful. He had to want children. He had to be a good and loving father. He had to enjoy books and music and pursuits of the mind. He had to make me laugh. I added a few more superficial things, including athleticism: I wanted to find you attractive. I wanted to *want* you, after all. And I did.

Yessirree, I did.

I often wonder if people attend their own funerals. This is the sort of useless, unanswerable koan that must drive atheists batty—not the questions themselves, but the fact that believers waste any time asking such things at all. Why the heck should it matter if you, Christopher Daniel Thomas Ringwald, plan to swoop in on your own services? Why the heck am I even thinking about it? And yet, I am thinking about it as I stand here in the receiving line at your wake, embracing friends and relatives and coworkers and neighbors and acquaintances— anyone who knew you well enough to know your spirit, your intellect, your greatness of love and moral fiber. The line of mourners is an hour long. The shiny young funeral director puts the head count at 400, possibly 100 more.

Our three brave children sweat it out beside me. Dear Mitchell is on crutches. The day after you died, while I was busy with funeral details, a brass door chime fell on his toe and all but severed it. Jane drove him to Urgent Care, where she was told, in more or less these words, "We don't do toes." She was about to schlep him to the E.R. when I suggested a podiatrist in the neighborhood, a funny, attractive man who had drained a cyst on my foot three days previous. Every neighborhood should have a foot doctor like him. I had eyeballed him with Jane in mind. I think I even mentioned him to you. Something like: Honey! The nicest podiatrist drained my big toe today, and he's sweet, and I have no idea if he's married, but assuming he *is* single, how do you suppose I could set him up with Jane? Huh? Got any ideas?

I don't recall what you said. At that point you were long past caring about such things. And she wound up meeting him, anyway.

Mitchell's in obvious pain. I try to get him to sit, but he refuses; like both of us, like all of us, he can be a stubborn piece of work. Loyal, too. He wants to stand for his father's wake, and nothing I say will dissuade him. After a couple of hours, Father Bob wanders over and asks about saying a few prayers; later, I learn that he and my dad have decided that Mitchell needs a break. So we sit. Father Bob speaks beautifully about love, then leads us all in the Lord's Prayer. Almost everyone ends it, as Catholics do, with ". . . deliver us from evil." But three or four voices carry on: "For thine is the kingdom, the power, and the glory."

Father Bob, a warm and splendid bear of a man with an infectious laugh, turns toward the few stray prayers. "Well," he cracks, "at least now we know who the *Protestants* are. . ." And this somber crowd ignites with laughter. I can't help wondering if you're laughing with us, and I think you must be. So much of your writing explored the shared ground between religions and — just as important to you — the differences that require a hard, true effort to understand. You never glossed over these. You never glossed over anything.

Ecumenism prevails the next day, the day of your funeral, which falls on Rosh Hashanah — the Jewish New Year. So many Jewish friends attend. One of them, Monique, grips my arm with love and urgency. "This is *Chris's* new year," she says. Baptists, Methodists, Episcopalians, Muslims, atheists are packed to the rafters alongside the hordes of Catholics. Thirteen priests concelebrate. Thirteen! Your brother, Carl, talks endearingly about driving you to the airport at 4 a.m. for a trip to Uganda. I talk about knowing it was you, you, you, from our very first date. For his homily, the deeply compassionate Father Chris speaks of your pain and goodness, the richness of your life, the torment in your soul. He tells a Buddhist parable about a man who's chased by a tiger off a cliff and, dangling from a branch, reaches for the sweetest fruit he's ever tasted.

The entire church choir has shown up to sing, the entire church band to play. Our impossibly courageous daughters stand alone, hold hands and sing Alicia Keys's "No One." A favorite of yours. They make it all the way through until the final measure, when they burst into tears—along with everyone else. I run up and hold them, stroking their hair. I imagine you're holding them, too. How I wish I could see that; how I wish I could observe you again with your children, see your arms around them, watch the love as it illumines and softens your face. I'll never again see it, but I'll always know it's there.

3 Social Security

My dad regards me again across the table. He taps it.

"You should call Social Security," he says. "You'll have some money coming to you."

Right.

"You should do that as soon as possible."

Right.

"I mean, as soon as possible. This week. Within the next few days. Today."

Right.

He taps again. He hums. This is his way of saying: I won't stop bugging you until you make that call. I won't leave you alone until you do whatever the fuck you need to do to get up and get moving forward.

And yes, if he were to vocalize this thought, he would be sure to include the word "fuck." He swears a lot.

Here I should note that my dad hasn't always been my dad. First, he was my headmaster, my teacher, my adviser, and my coach. Then, he became my friend Dan Richardson. Then, he and his wife, Pat, became my extra parents, and their kids became my bonus siblings. Then, they became the people who agreed to raise me and my sister, Lucy, in the event of our parents' deaths. ("The nice thing about Amy," he once told a friend, "is that if the right number of people die, she becomes my daughter.") Then, some years later, my sister killed herself and my parents died, all within a two-year span. My surrogate brother, Danny, then emailed me to say: "Consider my parents yours."

And that was that. The Richardsons all stopped being surrogate. They became my family, period. My dad became my dad. When he heard Chris had finally gone and killed himself after three hospitalizations and a catastrophic six-month bout of insomnia, anxiety, and depression, he packed up the Honda and drove to Albany. At home, his wife, Pat—my mom—was nursing a cold six weeks after a transplant operation, the kidney a gift from Danny. She couldn't come. But Dan did, huffing through the door like a shambling 6'2" blast of practicality, compassion, and hope.

On the Friday after my husband's death, under strict orders from Dad, I give Social Security a jingle. The exact course of the conversation I cannot later recall in detail, as I am dizzy with grief, sleep deprivation, and a permanent low-grade headache, but the fine gentleman at the other end spends about forty minutes feeding me questions. Some of these questions, most of them, are related to the children: their full names, birthdays, Social Security numbers, etc. etc. etc. Some of these questions are related to me. And Chris. And our marriage. And whether, in fact, it was a real and functioning marriage, not some sham operation designed to bilk Uncle Sam out of undeserved benefits.

So I tell the fine gentleman Chris's name. My name. Chris's birthday. My birthday. Our social security numbers. Chris's date of death. Then the fine gentleman starts getting personal. He asks how long we'd been married. Twenty years, I say. He asks for the date of our wedding. July 13, 1991, I say. He asks whether my husband and I were separated at the time of my husband's death. No, I say. He confirms that we were living together.

Yes, I say. Yes, yes, we were living together when he died. We were really, really seriously married, yes. Then, not missing a beat, the fine gentleman asks:

"Have you remarried?"

Uh.

Have I *remarried*? I repeat back at him.

"Yes, ma'am."

Um. Well. In the LAST...FOUR...DAYS?

And then I double over in an instant, body-shaking fit of belly laughter.

Then the fine gentleman says, "I'm sorry, ma'am, I had to ask." He continues to apologize over my guffaws, but there is no real cause; he just made my day. I tell him this between laughs — Hahahaha! You just made my day!! Hooo boy! Hahahahaha!! — because he obviously thinks I'm angry.

How could I be angry? Innocently, inadvertently, with a generosity of spirit disguised as a slavish bureaucratic mindset, this man has affirmed my place in the world and given me hope for the future. The idea that I could marry again, ever, is one of the more absurd notions to suggest to a woman whose husband has just leapt to his death from a parking garage. The idea that I might have tied the knot within ninety-six hours of such an event is somehow strangely affirming. Emphasize "strange." All the same: affirming.

My life isn't over.

4 Improvisation

The Sunday after Chris's funeral, our friends, Dennis and Kathy, host an evening of music. They invite every last soul who ever played with our neighborhood band, the Maraca Incident, so called because someone dropped one once and we must have spent a solid forty seconds sweeping up the beads. Before that, we went by Safety in Numbers, a reference to the band's large size, welcoming nature, and breezy attitude toward screw-ups. If anyone notices, no one cares. Chris wasn't a musician, but he was friends with all the band members, who knew him and loved him as the omnipresent, fiercely smart man-about-town with an old-school manner and a generous laugh. They're all mourning this loss. And so Dennis and Kathy open their home, fill their table with eats, and put extra chairs in their living room—and somehow, obeying some primal urge to gather and sing through our grief, everyone plays.

I carry my violin the block to their house and join them for an hour, maybe. That's all I can manage. But I have to manage something, if only to squawk out some tunes alongside a dozen people on guitar and ukulele and mandolin and banjo and electric bass and flute and, of course, maraca, and what else, you name it, anything that rattles sound through air with some measure of volume and joy. I squawk them out by ear because I always do, because I never have sheet music when I play with these folks. That's the thrill of it: flying by the seat of my pants, knowing I'll have to listen closely before I put down a finger and draw the bow.

What beauty and terror comes from improvising, because it's all an attempt to intuit the future—to hear where a melody's headed and then follow it by faith or by gut, or by the rules of Western music. It turns more beautiful and terrifying when Dennis, casually strumming his uke, turns to me in the middle of a song and blurts my name. He does this every single time we play, every single song. The "Amy!" means this: GO AHEAD AND IMPROVISE, MY FRIEND. Which I do, for several measures. But only after I panic first. And when the song is over I rib him, and he ribs me, and Kathy leans back with her bass around her neck and laughs. Everyone else does, too.

The friendship that comes from making music is mutually satisfying, mostly nonverbal, and deep. Singing and playing together yields an intimacy and connectivity based on something beyond words, and it's what I need right now. I also need to scare up the chutzpah to improvise, and not just here. I need to do it everywhere and always—to cock my ear forward, listening for the next tone in the sequence, finding and fingering some harmony that fits. Because whatever sheet of music I was following before, it's been swept away in the final gusting exhale of my husband's death. There's no more playing that song, ever. It's over. What comes next? I won't know until I hear it—and I somehow snatch the notes and play along.

Before I leave my friends tonight, we run through "Ashokan Farewell," Jay Ungar's aching waltz of valediction. It's our traditional goodbye to each other. It says everything that needs to be said this Sunday evening. It says goodbye to someone else. Its lilt is tinged with gratitude and sadness.

5 The Hall Pass

Already a week is gone without him. How'd that happen?

That first night, we bundled on the floor in sleeping bags and watched *Battlestar Galactica* until we couldn't. I didn't sleep, but Jeanne and Mitchell finally dropped off, and as they did, I lay there listening to their breathing, wondering what's in store for them and us. Something must be. I just don't know what. All previous plans have been summarily discarded. Whatever script or score I thought I was following has just been shredded, and improvisation is the order of the day. From now on, I'll be playing everything by ear. I'm winging it.

And I'm worrying—about the kids and their grief, and the effect of mine on theirs. Somehow, I've got to show them what it means to hurt but move through it, to bleed but keep going, to lose but live on. Can I? Will I? I worry about the increased risk of suicide rates in survivors. The children now qualify. I qualify doubly. And I can't do *that* to *them*. I express this concern to Alicia's husband, Joe, who calmly addresses the elephant in my living room from his spot on a wobbly loveseat.

"From one way of looking at it, no one in a ten-mile radius is more at risk of suicide," he says. "But from another way of looking at it, no one in a ten-mile radius is less at risk of suicide."

This helps. I remind myself, as Joe just has, that I'm bigger than all that happens to me—that I can take what lessons I choose from these events. The lesson I choose to take, the warning I see and hear and heed and mouth like a mantra, is: Just don't kill yourself. Show the kids that's not the way. The grief is a monster that can't be denied, but it needn't swallow everyone whole. If we let it rant and rage, and toss it a slab of meat when it shows up, it'll retreat—only for a moment, but the moments grow longer and the monster grows smaller in time.

Near the end of that first week, Jeanne's monster shows no sign of shrinking. She enters a deeper, blacker place of grieving, and asks if that's all there is. She doubts whether there's anything more. She questions both the existence of another life and the value of this one. She thinks her father must be dead and gone forever. She thinks she'll never see him again. But she needs to see him, she tells me. She regrets not saying goodbye the last morning he left for work. She wants to know if he's somewhere or nowhere, something or nothing, whole or demolished. And so, either way, whether he exists or not, she wants to be with him.

Be with him. There. If there's a There or not.

Be with him. In death.

She says all this. I hear all this and hold her and say things, all sorts of things, things that I know to be true, but she can't listen in her grief. So I hold her some more and then go shut myself in my bedroom, fall to my knees and say two burning prayers.

The first is to Chris:

Please, honey, visit Jeanne tonight. Go to her in a dream. Hug her. Tell her you're OK. Please. Please. Please.

The second is to God:

Please, God, let Chris go to Jeanne tonight. Give him permission to leave that world and return to this one, if only in a dream, and hug her and tell her he's all right. Please. Please. Please.

And then I go to bed. I sleep a bit, after a fashion. The next morning I'm at the kitchen sink, washing my cereal bowl, when Jeanne pads in.

"Mom," she says. "Mom, I had a dream."

Oh?

"I had a dream. About Dad. It seemed real. He seemed real."

Real?

"I walked into the kitchen. And I saw you bringing him in, and then I looked at him. He was wearing that blue checked polo shirt, the one with the pink lines. And his cargo shorts, you know?"

The green ones.

"Yeah. And he was smiling. And he was the real Dad, not the sick Dad. And I knew he was dead, but I knew he was real, too."

And. . .

"And I said, `Dad?' And then he smiled and said, `I'm all right now.' I hugged him, and he hugged me back the way he did when he was happy. And then he said, `I'm fine, I'm here.' And then I woke up."

Jeanne. Oh, Jeanne. Oh my God.

"Mom," Jeanne says. "It felt so real. Was it real?"

It was real, I say.

"How do you know?"

I tell her how I know. I tell her about my prayers to Dad and God, asking for a visit from the one and a hall pass from the Other. Because who knows how these things work? If the dearly departed could cross the divide just like that, easy-peasy, wouldn't they do so on a regular basis? Wouldn't our loved ones be popping by for visits all the time? The fact that they don't suggests it isn't exactly Standard Operating Procedure. This must require some special bureaucratic pre-approval.

All I know is I am relieved. Jeanne is out of her dark place, and when Madeleine and Mitchell wake and walk in and hear the story, they're envious: They, too, want a hug from Dad. I hate to disappoint them, but I don't expect he'll get another hall pass anytime soon.

Jeanne's dream is a gift for all of us, I say. Dad might not come to us in a dream again, but he'll make himself known in other ways. Maybe you'll hear a song on the radio. Maybe you'll just sense him near you, feel his love. But we take what gifts may come to us. And this is a big one, I tell them. This one is huge.

There in the kitchen, we embrace and chant a little verse that Chris made up. "The family hug," he called it.

Family hug, family hug,
We're having a family hug.
Hug a lot, bug a lot,
We're the family that hugs a lot.

In dreams and on waking, in that world and in this, we still are.

6 What I Do When I Do What I Do

"How are you?" the world wants to know, and to the world I say: OK. As well as can be expected, really. And the world then nods with love and sympathy. And the world wonders how I'm managing. And the world imagines me wailing and gnashing my teeth. And the world would be right. Minus the teeth part. I don't do anything with my teeth.

This is what I do when I grieve:

1) Cry.
2) Shout.
3) Cry and shout simultaneously.
4) Cry some more.
5) Cry while kicking things.
6) Cry while punching things.
7) Cry while kicking things, punching things, and yelling FUCK FUCK FUCK FUCK at the top of my lungs.
8) Cry while praying.
9) Cry while praying and yelling simultaneously (see FUCKs, above).
10) Cry until I run to the bathroom and disgorge stomach contents, and no, don't worry, I'm not bulimic, just systemically strung out.
11) Cry into a small but growing pool of mucus.
12) Cry while throwing a dictionary around the living room until the binding rips and the pages fly out and flutter to the floor.
13) Cry.

In ancient times, mourners rent their garments. I love that word "rent," but I can't say I've ever torn off my clothes in a public square in a mad fit of grief. That would involve displaying parts of my nekkid self I'd rather not display around others, whether they be others I know, or others I don't know. One way or the other, no garment-rending for moi. Just let me alone to writhe and weep into my own bodily seepage, and I'll be OK.

But "OK." What's "OK"? What is it that I'm claiming to be when I use that term? Am I saying that everything's hunky-dory? No. No hunky-doriness is anticipated any time soon, not in this life, not for me or anyone else. When I profess to be "OK," I'm putting myself somewhere on the giddiness spectrum between fabulous and sucky, probably suckier than not, with the tacit understanding that one's husband's recent suicide prevents one from achieving a state of high-functioning personal bliss. If I claimed to be much beyond "OK," no one would believe me. Maybe someday I'll shoot for "all right," or "fine," even. But for now: I'm OK. Feh.

What I'm saying, in other words, is: I have not yet curled up into a ball. I wake up. I brush my teeth. I get the kids off to school. I function. I eat when I remember. I laugh when I can. I go back to bed. I sleep, sort of. And in between, I take little breaks to:

14) Bawl my fucking eyes out.

7 The Casserole Club Has Now Come to Order

Alicia calls it "crisis ziti": the warm dish of pasta that lands on the porch in the aftermath of tragedy. Most folks assume lasagna is the go-to macaroni for mourning (there's even a passing joke about it in *We Bought a Zoo*), but Alicia and I are here to tell you it's ziti. Me, because I am at the receiving end. Alicia, because she put together the online calendar organizing the delivery of meals to our house for the next couple months. The kids and I love ziti, but even if we didn't, we'd be gobbling it up with gratitude. Every gift of time or food that comes our way is a reminder that we're not alone, no matter how badly we hurt, how often we stumble, or how gaping the hole left by Chris.

Most every night, Jane and her son, Maxim, arrive for dinner to help us eat. Some nights it is, indeed, ziti. Other nights it's pulled pork, or chicken and rice, or something creamy and salty and meaty and noodly simmering inside a pot. "It's another meeting of the Casserole Club," Jane pronounces one night, and we resolve to gather as often as we can. I like setting six places instead of four, which screams of Chris's truancy.

Quite a lot of that screaming goes on around the house these days: He was a neatnik, and I am not, and so every corner of my modest home is quickly accumulating crap. Every pile I see reminds me that the former resident crap-cleaner-upper is no longer with us. This pisses me off. I fight back an irrational urge to argue with him (Yeah! So the house is a mess! Ya gotta problem with that, Mr. Man?!!) before rolling up my sleeves and sweeping, mopping, picking at stacks of clutter. I set the bar very low. When the kitchen floor crunches, that's my cue.

I explain this to my friend Bob, one of the people I now rely upon to laugh with me at my misery. This has become a critical test of friendship, lately. No one lacking in morbid humor need apply. Bob has lots; sometimes I call him up just to hear his sides split. So I tell him about the latest meeting of the Casserole Club, at which the children, Jane, Maxim, and I discussed the precise wording of my epitaph.

Not Chris's epitaph. Mine.

Working out the details of Chris's headstone was straightforward enough. We chose the cemetery (wooded and quiet), then the grave (to fit two urns), then the style and size (flat, in the ground, double), then the border (plain), then the emblems (roses and a crucifix) and then, most importantly, the wording under his name. After a brief discussion, the children and I agreed on "Dad, Husband, Light of Our Lives," which captured everything everyone wanted to say.

A much more challenging task was figuring out what to say under my half of the monument. Why it needed to say anything, beyond my name and D.O.B., escaped me until I broached the subject with the woman in charge of memorials. And then it still escaped me.

I said: Ummm, why do we need to figure out a motto for me?

She said: Well, you need to do that now.

I said: Ummm, why?

She said: Well, because you can't do that later.

I said: Ummm, why not?

She said: Well, it's not stone, so it can't be carved. It's bronze. So if you don't do it now, your children will have to have a bronze plate made up and riveted onto the marker.

I said: Ummm, what's wrong with that?

She said: Well, they'll already have to attach a bronze plate with your date of death. So this would be another plate. A second plate. It would be expensive. Your children would have to pay for it. And the marker would be covered with all these additional plates and rivets.

I said: Ummm.

I thought about this for a moment, trying to picture a Frankenstein's monster of ugly, slapdash, bolted metalwork.

While I was thinking, she added: Also, this can be something you can share now with your children. Talk to them about it. Ask them what they want on your memorial. You'd be surprised how healing this sort of conversation can be.

I said: Ummm. Healing. Ummm.

And so, later that night, I broached the subject with the Casserole Club: OK, kids! What should we put on my half of the headstone? The lady at the cemetery wants to know!

They found this notion highly entertaining. I have to hand it to them: Contemplating their mother's death many decades (one prays) in the future did not seem to phase them *at all*. Their only worry was that I might wind up short-shrifted: there wasn't that much room, they didn't want to repeat the phrasing for Chris, and there are only so many heartfelt filial aphorisms you can squeeze into half a dozen words.

So what about: "Well, That's Over With."

Or how about: "She Got Through Shit."

Or my favorite (borrowing from Monty Python): "I'm Not Dead Yet!"

Of the three kids, Madeleine was the most concerned that I get the wording exactly right ("This will be on your grave *forever*"), Jeanne, the most witheringly ironic ("That would be SHOCKING to bolt on an extra plate, like, SHOCKING"), Mitchell, the most on-point ("Let's just say `Bye, Mom!' — with a quickie wave of the hand). Meanwhile, Jane and Maxim laughed into their turkey casserole, or some other edible gift we chowed down on that night.

Finally, we settled on the phrase that will sit atop my ashes for perpetuity: "Loving Mother, Loving Wife." The kids OK'd it, but didn't much like it. Too blah, but whatev. It included all the necessary facts and sentiments.

The possibility that I might, at the time of my death, be married to someone else didn't even cross my mind. Because it wasn't a possibility. It *couldn't* be a possibility. Anyway, a death requires the living to make all sorts of decisions when they're in no shape to make them, and this decision's not too bad. Or so I think, until I start explaining to family and friends that I am soon to be fully memorialized in bronze.

When I tell my dad, his reaction is: "OK, Ames. But that is really fucking weird."

When I tell Pam, her reaction is: "????" With a touch of: "!!!!!" And then a reiteration of: "?????"

When I tell Bob, his reaction is: "What? WHAT??! You mean, if I visit Chris's grave, I'll see a memorial for YOU, TOO?" And then he says again: "WHAT??!!" Finally he says, and here I am quoting him in full: "HAHAHAHAHAHAHAHAHA!!" Bob has a giant laugh. It almost breaks the phone, and I love him for it.

And I remark to myself, You are truly friends with right people, *chiquita!* People who laugh propulsively at your headstone and much-anticipated death!

When I explain the situation to Chris's brothers and sisters, they are unfailingly, stunningly sweet—because they are unfailingly, stunningly sweet all the time, no matter what, even when my concerned brother-in-law, Tom, grabs me by the hands at Chris's burial and complains that I'm stubborn for not accepting help. Then, when he apologizes for saying this, he is unfailingly, stunningly sweet.

He's right. I am one stubborn broad. But I'm also a lucky broad, rich with love and sated by laughter. Plus ziti.

8 Two, Two, Two People at Once

I am a film critic. I am the person people loathe when they see a movie they love or hate and then surf over to Rotten Tomatoes to see what the critics thought, and they find a critic who hated the movie they loved or loved the movie they hated, and so this critic, to them, is the Scum of the Earth. I am also the person people adore when they love or hate a movie and surf onto Rotten Tomatoes and find that every critic disagrees with them but me, and so, to them, I am the Best Critic Ever.

Some weeks I am the Scum of the Earth and the Best Critic Ever simultaneously. I am accustomed to that. In addition, I am accustomed to being informed by readers that I'm a woman, and while I've never been accused of being a man, I have, at various times, been told that I am: a right-winger (not true); a pinko (sort of true); a Catholic (true); an anti-Catholic (not true); an outraged suburbanite (not true); an amoral urbanite (half true); a Texan (not true); a Yankee (true); and a shill for the movie studios (but where's the lucre, pardner?). I've also been told I'm an oldster, a youngster, a pointy-nosed snob, and a talentless hack who "shouldn't give up (my) day job." Which I find amusing, because this *is* my day job, buster.

And because it's my day job, this is the work to which I return after two weeks of full-time mourning. Watching a Jack Black/Steve Martin movie in an all-but-empty theater at 10 a.m. on a weekday is strange enough. Watching a Jack Black/Steve Martin movie in an all-but-empty theater at 10 a.m. a whole fourteen days after my husband's suicide is downright hypnagogic, more so if the Jack Black/Steve Martin movie at issue concerns competitive birders. Before being assigned to this film, I hadn't known there were such things as competitive birders. It seems ridiculous.

But then, everything seems ridiculous to me now. It's hard for me to treat anything short of grave illness and death as a pressing or important issue. Nothing beyond the bottom line — being alive and well, and knowing my loved ones are alive and well — means that much to me any longer. I do my job because it's my job, and I enjoy it. I know I get paid to file clean, lively copy on deadline, and getting paid is an important part of feeding my children. So I watch this gentle, harmless film. I take notes on bird species (buffleheads and grosbeaks!). I enjoy the travel scenery (Aleutians and the Gulf of Mexico!), and I laugh at Martin's trademark rubbery dance moves.

But not one second of its 100-minute running time passes unmolested by memories of Chris's death. I am aware of him, it, everything, all of the time. It eats my brain. I feel as though I'm occupying parallel bodies in parallel universes. In the first universe, Amy One is laughing and functional, and possibly even joyous. In the other universe, Amy Two is consumed by grief. Amy One is singing alto in a church choir, playing violin in a community orchestra, or fiddling it up with friends in a neighborhood band; meanwhile, Amy Two is silently howling, her twisted mouth aping the screamer in Edvard Munch's *Der Shrei*. Both of these worlds, both of these Amys, are authentic. Both demand my attention. I'm present; my husband is gone. Grieving means honoring both realities at once.

Lo, I am Scum of the Earth. I am the Best Critic Ever.

9 And Now, a Few Words about Guilt

Friends and family tell me I shouldn't feel guilty. I love them for believing this, I'm grateful to them, I consider myself blessed to have such people saying such things, but it's bullshit. Of course I should feel guilty; I'm the person who stood up in church and promised to love and hold Chris to my dying breath, and I failed on both counts. I tried, but I failed. I loved him as best and as fully as I could, but I didn't love him enough to keep him alive.

Friends and family tell me I couldn't keep him alive. This isn't bullshit; they are correct. I learned from my sister's illness and suicide that you can't love someone back to health. You can't prevent people from killing themselves, not unless you chain yourself to their wrists and follow them around. Even then, they'd find a way.

So I know, intellectually, that my husband's death is not my fault. I know, intellectually, that I tried my damnedest to keep him engaged and reel him back among the living. I know I loved him. And yet I feel guilty. I will always feel guilty. Those who tell me I shouldn't feel guilty are telling me this out of love, and acceptance, and a timeworn knowledge of my propensity for self-flagellation, out of the sincere conviction that I'm blameless, and out of deep concern for my well-being and the well-being of my children. It's better for the kids if I shed the guilt. I know that, too. But I'm feeling it.

I knew that I would. I felt guilty after my sister killed herself. I felt guilty as a kid after my late father made an attempt. I knew from the first minute of the first day that I would feel guilty over my husband's death, and I knew that the people closest to me would tell me that I shouldn't. But guilt is an unavoidable facet of grief in the aftermath of suicide. It's part of the pain, and since when does anyone have control over how they badly hurt, and where? Osteoarthritis clots my lower back. When the pain flares up I gulp back analgesics and soldier on as best I can, but no one tells me I shouldn't feel it. No one tells me it shouldn't hurt.

It should hurt! It should. My husband's death is a violation. . It's an outrage. It's a betrayal of all the plans we'd made, an affront to our vows, a breach in the order of things and a bloody dismemberment of the sacred and sexual body we formed together. I don't blame him for this—I don't blame him for losing his sleep and his mind and his grip on the world—and I don't believe he made a conscious "choice" to jump. But he did jump. And I didn't. I'm still here. As the one left behind, I feel the weight of living and the burden of knowing that sometimes, in this imperfect universe, with our imperfect hearts, there's a limit to what love can do. We believe it to be limitless, and so we must, or we would never have the guts and faith to marry. My love had a limit. My love was not enough.

I feel guilty.

10 Holy Shit

For some reason, Chris hated the word "shit." He hated to hear me say it, and rarely said it himself. I threatened to title a previous book "Holy Shit," considering it a cute play on the deeply religious yet craptacularly tragic aspects of my childhood family's story, but he blanched. Just the thought of it gave him pains. So of course, in the months leading up to his death and in the months that have followed, this singularly potent single-syllable word has come to define my life.

First, "shit magnet." This phrase was coined by my Richardson brother, Randy, to describe one who exerts a powerful gravitational force on all that stinks: medical shit, job shit, unlucky-in-love shit, you-name-it shit. The closest synonym is probably *schlimazel*, the Yiddish word for the poor schlub most likely to have soup spilled into his lap; the spiller is a *schlemiel*, which, I suppose, Randy might term a "shit dispenser." The Richardsons are shit magnets of the first order (that's a whole other book, and my adoptive Dan-Dad plans to write it), but they are the most cheerful and loving shit magnets you will ever, ever meet. The shit flies at them, but they wipe it off with a smile.

My husband's illness was shit that made no sense to anyone: not to me, not to his friends and family, certainly not to him. For more than twenty years he was the sanest man I'd ever known, and then he wasn't. His personality changed. He stopped sleeping. Ambien kept him awake all night. Psych meds were no help either, and his hospitalizations only made him worse. After one long, awful day when he disappeared and I

called the police, he was compelled to enter a psychiatric crisis
center, and I was compelled to sit down with the doctor and his
team to determine whether Chris was at risk for suicide. They
asked me if I understood the danger. I said yes. I told them
about my sister's suicide in 1992, and my father's attempt in
1974. I knew what this meant, I assured them.

"Oh," remarked the psychiatrist. "So you're a survivor."

Yeah, I said. Or you could just call me a shit magnet.

And darned if they didn't all laugh.

My brother-in-law, Murray, sits in my kitchen and says it
flat-out: "You're not a hex."

My turn to laugh.

"You'll be tempted to think that you're a hex, that this is
your fault, all this suicide. But you're not. It's not."

I know, I say. I keep telling myself that. Thank you. I know.

But what I want to say, not to Murray but to the universe at
large, is: WHAT THE FUCK IS GOING ON HERE? ARE YOU
FUCKETY-FUCKING KIDDING ME? ANOTHER SUICIDE?
SERIOUSLY?

And so I encounter the toughest shit yet: figuring out how
to process my husband's fatal leap so that I and my children and
all whom I treasure in this world won't lose our collective minds
with grief and remorse. I know that I'm the crux of it; I have to
frame this outrageous rearrangement of our lives in a way that
allows all of us to move forever forward with love and hope, or
something like it. And what I figure out is this: It can't be figured
out. Chris's madness and suicide will never make sense. We will
never understand it. My friend Jo calls it a "sorrowful mystery,"
and I agree—realizing, finally, that I can only comprehend his
death as something incomprehensible.

I share this thought with the kids. They absorb it quickly
and completely, having witnessed the six-month change in their
father and accepted the fact that their "real" dad, their *well* dad,

didn't choose to leave them and this life. Children are deeper than adults, wiser, because they're accustomed to not having all the information. They already know they can't know everything.

We discuss this not-knowing at the Casserole Club one night. I tell them our brains aren't big enough to grasp what happened. I tell them someday we might, but not now. Not in the land of the living.

That's when Jeanne hits us with it. Profundity from the mouth of a teenager. "While we're alive, and we want to understand it, we can't," she says. "When we're dead, and we'll be able to understand it, we won't give two shits."

To that I say, amen.

Later, I think about the shitness of it all, and the mystery inherent in the shitness. What a worrier I am. How I fret over my shortcomings, past, present, and future. I ask myself what might have happened, what should be happening, what will. I have no clue what to do with myself now, stripped from the ballast of my husband and tossed adrift in some new direction on waters foaming with uncertainty and pain. I'm no longer his wife, but the whole notion of widowhood gives me *agita*: it's a state of being defined by a vacancy. I'm more than unmarried, and I'm not quite whole.

Why did he have to die? Who am I without him beside me? The fuck if I know. I am obviously suffering through an existential crisis.

As I said. Shit.

11 In Which I Begin to Resemble Alaskan Wildlife

Gripped in the insanity of grief and recurring guilt, I decide I will never know a man biblically again. I don't want to. I don't deserve to. Not after losing the mate of my dreams. Not after failing to love him and heal him and bring him back to me, to us, to life. So no physical intimacy. Nope. Not with anyone. Ever.

I consider becoming a nun. This is not a totally bananas concept, and it's not totally out of character, either. I am Catholic. I do pray quite a bit. Plus, I've known a lot of nuns over the years, and they are all cool people, and one of the coolest used to birth lambs every spring, and I like the idea of serving the Lord and the poor and living a more contemplative life, although I'd rather not have to wear a habit in the middle of August. Of course none of this constitutes what's generally meant by a "calling," but it nevertheless wings through my head. Other things wing, too. Such as: Hmmm, Mitchell will graduate eventually...I'll be an empty-nester...I'll need something to occupy my time...I took a year of Latin in high school. . . I like sheep...and I'm never having sex again, anyway. So it could work!

I have several years to sort out the details of this monumental career change. In the meantime, I stop shaving my legs. This isn't so much a decision as a passive and unconscious form of self-mortification, much like failing to bathe or forgetting to brush my hair until it's all matted and dreadlocky, and I am inspired to sing Bob Marley songs while stoned and wearing a large knit hat. That might be fun. Though I've never smoked pot. Really! I've never smoked pot! Who else do you know who can say that without their pants spontaneously combusting! That, too, should prepare me well for the nunnery, that is, the inexperience with the pot, not the pants, although I'd bet there are one or two nuns bred in the 60s who might have inhaled a puff before they took their vows.

Am I, indeed, prepared to do such a thing? Probably not. But it seems like a good idea for now, certainly a better idea than gettin' down n' dirty with some fella who isn't Chris. From where I stand, that is no idea at all.

Now, before I delve any further into this leg-shaving business, I need to ask: Are you Italian? Even the itsiest bit? Because if you are, or if you're married to someone who is, or if you once had a hippie high-school English teacher who wore peasant dresses who was, then you can skip to the next chapter. Because you already know what's coming. If not, read on.

Italians grow hair. All over their bodies. This is what we do, and we're really good at it. I'd go so far as to deem it a calling, much like becoming a nun. This isn't a problem for the men, because no one looks at a man with hairy legs or armpits and thinks, Blecccchhh! Why doesn't he clear-cut that jungle?! Even in the era of metrosexual manscaping, it is still acceptable for a fellow to appear in public with a pelt of long, curly filaments.

But a woman. If a woman does the same, she risks disgrace. Those who see her unshaved make the following assumptions: 1) that she's European; 2) that she's from Woodstock, New York; 3) that she just awoke from a forty-year nap; 4) that she forgot she has legs; 5) that she's from Woodstock, Vermont; 6) that she forgot she has armpits; 7) that she's from anywhere else in Vermont; 8) that she just doesn't give a shit; 9) that her obsession with patchouli doesn't leave time for sex; 10) that she left her razor in a hemp backpack at the organic food co-op; 11) that her husband just died and she's planning to become a nun.

No one actually sees my hairy legs. This is fortunate, because they go from sleek 'n sexy to hairy 'n disgusting in what seems like minutes flat. At 9:00 a.m. I am a lustrous feminine vision. By 9:03 I am covered in a wiry pileous thicket that could be used to scrub pots. Heeding my better nature, I refrain from climbing into the sink to give this a go.

But what to do? I mean, with the legs. The legs require some sort of camouflaging. Fortunately, this is autumn, and the air is now cool enough to stop wearing shorts without drawing suspicion. But I like to wear skirts and dresses to church, because, once a week, I like to feel like a girl. The rest of the week I feel like a movie critic who writes from home, which I'm sad to say is not the same as feeling like a girl, because it involves a lot of baggy T-shirts from the Clinton era. I am also sad to say that as large as they are, they do not reach all the way to my toes.

Even if they did, I wouldn't wear them to church. So I wear slacks. Black slacks. Sometimes dark gray slacks. I don't own anything colorful in the slacks department, or in any department. Jeanne, a fashionable creature who inherited her knack for shopping and dressing from some part of the gene pool unrelated to me, is always after me to go wild and snazz up my wardrobe with non-funereal tones. This was true even before Chris died, and it's truer now.

"Mom!" she says as I prepare to head out one Sunday morning. "Mom! Don't wear black!"

I like black, I say.

"Mom!"

But I was born in New York City. I have to wear black. It's required. Says so right on my birth certificate—see?

"Mom!"

OK, OK, I won't wear black.

Fortunately, I have a couple of handy-dandy leg-obscuring ankle-length skirts, and one of them is red. But I can't wear it every week, or I will begin to feel like the closing ceremonies of the Beijing Olympics. So the children order me to go shopping for clothes. Colorful clothes, they stipulate. No black allowed. My in-laws give me a lovely cream-colored sweater and a velvety blue scarf. Jeanne orders me to wear them. She orders me to wear lots of things, and I dutifully don them and venture forth in public.

And as I do, none but I know the secret that lurks beneath my clothes, a silent killer that rises from the depths (or at any rate, my dermis) and attacks my self-esteem. I'm still not shaving my legs. I'm still not doing the deed—with anyone, ever again. Lifelong celibacy seems like a radical option, but it's easier than figuring out how to be a single woman in the wake of my husband's suicide. Too much effort; I'd rather not try. Thus I make my decision. From now on, depilatories be damned! Sex with nobody! Here, here!

Now pass me a comb and a scrunchie, so I can braid my legs.

12 The Things I'm Not

Still don't know who I am, yet. Still not sure what it means to even know who I am. Knowing how to define myself and my reality and how to move through it: that's a thing of the distant past, back in the olden days when I occupied that cozy, coupled place in the spheres reserved for the happily married. I'm not there. I'm not in the single world, either. Right now I reside in negative space; I'm less than something. When will I feel like anything, again? When will I even want to?

What follows is an itemized list of the things that I'm not. I'm putting quotes around them because they are, coincidentally, the things I'm most often told that I am:

"Strong."

"Amazing."

"Inspiring."

"Incredible"

"So strong."

"So amazing."

"So inspiring."

"So incredible."

"So amazingly strong."

"So amazingly inspiring."

"So amazingly incredible"

"So incredibly strong."

"So incredibly amazing."

"So incredibly inspiring."

"So amazingly and incredibly strong and inspiring."

"So stramazincrediblizing."

Supposedly I am all of these things, and all at the same time. Another thing I purportedly am: a source of awe and admiration. Folks often tell me how much they admire me, and it's tough to hear, because I don't admire myself much. To admire oneself, one must have a grasp on what one's self actually is. One needs a target. Narcissus would have been nothing, just another cute boy with bad manners, had he not caught a glimpse of his face in the pond.

Here's another thing I hear: "I don't know how you do it."

People say this to me all the time. I never know how to reply, because I don't know what "it" is, and whatever "it" is, I'm pretty sure I'm not actually doing it. Because I don't believe I'm actually doing *any*thing, other than moving through each day in a blur that breaks for periodic trays of ziti and cyclical trips to the bathroom.

So this is how I usually respond: Uhhh...I dunno. I just...I just...I just...ahmmmm...you know, like...sort of...ummm...errrrr...nrrrhgghsppllt??

More often than not, the descent into nonsensical consonant-spitting brings an end to conversation.

I have an easier time responding to this variation: "I don't know how you get out of bed in the morning." See, that one makes sense to me. It's a solid and incisive observation of my new reality; the person saying it recognizes that, logically, I should be knotted in the fetal position, whimpering into my kneecaps, instead of walking around and talking to people and pretending I'm, like, normal or something. Because everyone knows I'm not normal. *I* know I'm not normal. So when they say this, I just laugh and say: Yeah, right?! I don't know how I get out of bed, either. But I do. Because I have to.

Another word I often hear is "grace." When I hear this one, I think: Like I have any! Ha! Have you seen me *walk*, babycakes? I'm pigeon-toed, for crying out loud. As a soccer player, I was quick enough and tough enough and knew well enough how to jive with the ball, but I was never graceful, never one who rolled through space with an air of fluid destiny. I know, I know, I'm being too literal. But even in the poetic sense, I am the klutz who klunks through life.

Chris used to tell a story on himself, a little one uncorked with big laughs, about a trek across a snowy yard at the Adirondack home of my aunt and uncle. It was the middle of a long, hard winter, and the power had gone out, and Chris, wanting to be helpful, offered to assist Uncle Allie with the generator. So the pair of them—my slim uncle and my thickly built husband—crossed a blanket of snow glazed with ice. Allie minced lightly on top of its skin. Chris clomped and stomped through the ice behind him, *ker-smash, ker-smash, ker-smash.*

I wasn't there to witness this scene, but it plays like a memory for me; I've plodded through enough crusty snow over the years to know how it feels. I've never been an elegant mincer, whether trodding ice or emotions. I *ker-smash.*

Grace isn't mine, not now, not ever, regardless what people say. Awkwardness and ineptitude are all I have to assist me on this trip, wherever it takes me. But I don't know. Maybe being inept, or uninspiring, or a credible human mess isn't such a bad thing at this stage in the game. What helps me most is accepting that I'm weak. And I think it helps the kids, too. They worry about me, and I worry about them worrying about me, but what good would it do them if I wore a stoic face and an A-line dress and busied myself by baking brownies while whistling the theme from *Donna Reed*? They'd probably worry *more.* They'd think I was abducted and replaced by helmet-haired visitors from the planet Zplork.

My offspring witness me, sometimes, in the midst of secreting body fluids. It would be a touch screwy if they didn't, as I'd always be running to the attic storage room to howl and honk my nose in the dark. Besides, I want them to feel okay about their own grief; I want them to know that howling and nose-honking are perfectly sane coping mechanisms. "I'm just having a moment," I tell them. "We all have moments." I then eject more snot and tears, wishing my husband back. He doesn't come.

When I'm all done crying, a blessed stillness descends for just a moment. In that moment I don't feel graceful, but I do feel grace: a peace and a presence greater than myself. This I greet as the Holy Spirit, the God who drops by uninvited—always with perfect timing, never without a caress on the back and a warming plate of cookies. Both the rub and the baked goods say, Yep, Ame-o, this whole thing sucks, but at least there's life and chocolate.

That kind of grace is the sweetness in the air, the whiff of living that drifts and calms. And there are times when I do have that.

13 The Lasts

On the morning of September 11, 2001, I was rolling baby Mitchell through the neighborhood after dropping the girls at school. It was a beautiful, brilliant, crystalline morning, the sky lightly tufted with clouds. I heard the distant shriek of a plane at high altitude, and I pointed to it.

Look up there, Mitchell! Look!

I squatted beside my alert one-year-old in an umbrella stroller, and we took a few moments to trace the fat white contrail streaking across the blue. See that, pumpkin? See it?

I often think about that plane. No, it wasn't one of *the* planes that crashed and stole so many lives that day, but it was the last plane I saw before I heard the news. Maybe it was the last plane that streaked over Albany that day. It was, more than that, the last plane I ever greeted with childlike excitement, for every plane thereafter became freighted with the grief of 9/11. Looking back, I recognized this one plane as a marker of sorts, a distinct visual coda that declared an end to innocence.

Life is full of such markers. But we can only see them in retrospect. After my sister died, I remembered my last conversation with her (pained). The last birthday gift I sent her (a colorful fabric horse, hastily wrapped). The last hug we shared (at Christmas). Had I known these would be the last conversation, gift, hug, I would never have stopped talking to her. I would have sent her endless gifts. I would have hugged and hugged and hugged her until forcibly pried apart. But we can't live that way, knowing everything to come, or we would never move on to the next thing. And there's always a next thing. There has to be. Without a next thing, we're static and lost.

But in the worst of grief, the nexts don't matter. It's the lasts that do. I replay, like a constant video loop, my last kiss with Chris: in the kitchen, just before he left that morning. I recall the last lunch I made for him. The last prayer I said with him (the Our Father). The last massage I gave him. The last dinner we ate as a family. The last Mass we attended. Our last hug as a family of five. Our last time dancing—at my cousin Jackie's wedding in Pennsylvania. Our last time camping—at Nickerson State Park on Cape Cod. The last movie we saw together (*Super 8*). The last time we made love.

Some lasts I can't remember. The last time he walked in happy after a day's work. The last time I spied him walking down the street in a long coat and fedora, swinging an umbrella. The last time he threw me a grin and said, "Hello, beautiful!" The last time he gave himself a wedgie and waddled around laughing. The last time he asked me to read something he'd written. The last time we talked about a book. The last time I heard him reading to Mitchell, his voice rising and dipping in sing-song cadences. Their last bout of wrestling on the living room floor.

His last bike ride. Our last card game. His last kayak. Our last walk.

The lasts will drive me batshit, if I let them. I berate myself: I should have kissed him longer! Embraced him harder! I should never have let go! I should have hung onto those moments forever and ever! As though any moment can go on forever and ever, whether we grasp their significance or not. Even if it could, even if we did, it wouldn't matter, because living isn't living without movement. We'd stop at one memory and never get past it to form another. If I hadn't let go of Chris that last time, if I hadn't broken away and continued on through life, I would still be locked in that final clinch between us. And if I were, he might still be here, but nothing else would. I would have no time or love or presence of mind for anything or anyone beyond it. Not even my children.

So I'm grateful for my lasts with Chris. I'm glad I loved him and knew him well and long enough to accumulate so many. I wish I could have accumulated more. But now I'm onto the nexts, and then the nexts, and then the nexts, until, someday, the nexts become lasts for someone else—and I'm finally done with living.

14 F.S.O., Part I

Before long, I come to realize that Figuring Shit Out is the central and ceaseless work of widowhood. F.S.O. becomes my new M.O.

During the first week (or, The Week, as the kids and I now call it), everyone else figured shit out for me—cooked for me, thought for me, led me around by the hand, cleaned my house, organized my fridge.

But at some point, the newborn widow needs to figure out shit on her own. She needs to do this because, no matter how helpful friends and family and neighbors are, no matter how grateful she is to them, no matter how reliable they are in providing food or housework or advice, she simply can't bank on them to be there 24/7. Friends of mine offer up their husbands to help fix and haul things, but what if I need something fixed or hauled at 2 a.m.? I'd damn well better to be able to fix it or haul it myself.

Therefore, one of the first and most fundamental laws of F.S.O. is this: Only pack a bag that I can carry alone. Literally and figuratively, to the extent that I can, I must limit my burdens to those I can bear without a husband.

So that heavy kayak he liked to take out onto the Hudson and the Normanskill? Can't get it up on the roof of the car by myself. I may as well give it away and get a lighter one. And that Thule rooftop bullet carrier Chris would whip on and off of vehicles without a hand from me? Too fucking heavy. Useless to me. I'll have to buy a soft carrier instead.

I am not a weakling, as women go. I have sturdy legs ("thunder thighs," we called them in soccer), strong arms and a stubborn disposition. But my husband had fifty pounds of brawn on me, and he isn't here. I no longer have a masculine musclehead to love and assist me in the conveyance of very large objects, and so: Go, go, go! F.S.O.!

Shit I've figured out so far includes:

- How to jump a dead car battery alone;
- How to sump-pump six inches of water from a flooded basement alone;
- How to install the storm windows on an 87-year-old house alone;
- How to carry a ping-pong table up two flights of stairs (granted, this was incredibly stupid) alone;
- How to repair doorknobs on an 87-year-old house alone;
- How to build a not-totally-lame fire alone;
- How to prune a row of bushes two feet taller than I am alone;
- How to use a power screwdriver in assembling furniture out of a box (people, be sure the bit is set to rotate clockwise!) alone; and, last but not least. . .
- How to store the Tupperware so it doesn't fall on my head. Alone.

That final one needs to be explained. My husband didn't tower over me, but four inches is a critical height deferential when it comes to the storage of kitchen items in the cabinet above the fridge. I loved the man passionately. He was good, faithful, smart, loving, jovial, hilarious. But he refused to store the Tupperware anywhere but in that one blasted cabinet.

For 18 years, we lived together in this house. For 18 years, he insisted that the food containers fit perfectly up there so long as one took the time to arrange them according to size. For 18 years, he demonstrated for me—the less organized one, the shorter one, the slobbier one—the ideal Tupperware stacking methods that would liberate me and free the kitchen of clutter. For 18 years, he suggested I pull over a stool or a chair when I remove and return plastic food containers to the cabinet, as it was just a smidge too high for me to reach without it. For 18 years, I failed to pull over a stool or a chair. And for 18 years, every day, no matter what, whenever I reached into that cabinet, the motherfucking Tupperware fell on my head.

This phenomenon continues for several weeks after his suicide. Old habits die hard. I open the cabinet to pull out an item, and the Tupperware falls on my head. I open the cabinet to return an item, and the Tupperware falls on my head. The Tupperware falls on my head at morning, noon, and night. It falls on my head when I am alone and when I am with people. It falls on my head when I'm tired or well-rested, hurried or relaxed, sobbing or laughing, listening to *All Things Considered*, or silently rehashing the final season of *Lost*.

Until, one day, it hits me: I can move the Tupperware! I can defeat it! I have the power within me! F.S.O.! Bwahahahaha!

Jane, a witness to many brutally shocking Tupperware head attacks, watches one evening, pre-Casserole Club, as I assiduously move the containers from their lofty realm into a lower one, beneath the microwave—down at ankle-level, with the proletarian crowd of pots and pans. "Wow wow wow! I can't believe you're doing this!" she yells in affirmation. The process takes all of twenty minutes. I wonder why I've never attempted this before.

Then I remember: Because it wasn't worth a fight. Chris mattered more to me, way more, than the mild trauma of having a bunch of plastic vessels peg me in the noodle once or twice a day. As he always said, "The trick isn't finding the person you can live with, but the person you can't live without." Or, to quote my late mother, "People come in packages." Including Tupperware.

15 Lost in Space

How do I go about this? How do I live the rest of my life without him? Those dreams we shared—they all hurt, even the vaguest ones, the goofiest ones, the dreamiest ones. At the start of our marriage, we promised to buy a convertible after our last kid had left for college. Will I still buy one without Chris? The older couples who stroll around our neighborhood, some of them hand in hand, others cinched by the intangible bond of years between them: We had planned to join them someday. We had planned to *be* them someday. Will I now walk the neighborhood alone?

All I know is I can't stop walking. Neighbors drop by to air me out, take me around. I can't stop living—or loving, either, whether I become a nun or not. The love that surrounds and carries us reminds me, in the worst of my mourning, that love is, in fact, the only answer. I can't respond to death and despair with death and despair; I must respond with life and love. Any other response will only lead us further into darkness.

From a pile of scrap paper I pull out a wrinkled blue sheet and tear it in half. With a black Sharpie, I make my list—a tally of directives for the rest of my life. How to go on. What to do. I would like to say I arrive at this list following days of meditation, or rumination, or prayer, but I do not. It simply spills out. Everything about it feels self-evident, compulsory.

I write:

LIVE.

GIVE.

LOVE.

LAUGH.
GROW.
LEARN.
PRAY.
BE GRATEFUL.
BE PRESENT.
MAKE MUSIC.
HAVE FAITH, and
STAND UP STRAIGHT!!

Then, as an afterthought, in the corner I scribble: (ALSO: EXERCISE). Then I stick it on the fridge at eye-level. I read it over a few times. Yup, that says it all. It works.

Chris took up more space than other people; I don't know how else to put it. Due to an unusual and potent blend of confidence, charisma, and sheer intellectual dynamism, he had the presence of a much larger man. He entered a room and filled it. He jumped into a conversation and commanded it. I more than loved him; I was consumed by him, seduced by his vitality and thrilled by what I always called (to myself alone) the "muchness" of him.

His abrupt departure has sucked the air out of our lives, creating a vacuum. The house's population, down from five to four, seems to have dwindled even further. Everything is out of proportion. The bed is too wide. The meals are too small. The trash is too light. And the van is way too big.

I hate it, anyway. It's piss-poor in snow, as I discovered last winter when I twice got stuck in snow banks and failed to extract myself without assistance—something that hadn't happened to me in thirty years. As any denizen of the North will tell you, being able to rock yourself free from a bank is an important acquired skill. If you can't do that unaided, you may as well move to Orlando. Since I don't want to move to Orlando,

I need to get a new car. Littler. Easier to handle. Better in snow. Better suited to our downsized lives.

And so, in the F.S.O. sub-category of Figuring Vehicular Shit Out, I decide to trade in the van for a 2009 all-wheel-drive Toyota Matrix, which I purchase from a ginormous suburban dealership north of Albany. The young woman who sells it to me is chirpy and charming and helpful. On the day I breeze in to pick up my car, she asks if I'd like to have my picture taken with it.

With it?

"Yes!" she says.

You mean, with the car?

"Yes! To remember the day!"

Ahhhmmm, I say. And then I think: Do I NEED to remember the day? If I forget the day, will I live the rest of my life saddled with regret, shedding bitter tears? But she seems like a sweet kid. She wants to take my photo, and no harm in that. Let her.

I pose before my hot new wheels and smile as she snaps, remembering not to close my eyes (I am an incurable blinker) but forgetting to remove my raincoat. You'd think the raincoat wouldn't make a difference. But it does make a difference. Because the raincoat was Chris's, so it's big on me. And it's red. And my pants are black. And the car is black, too. And when I receive the photo in the mail a week later, I appear as a legless blob of cherry brilliance against a pitch-dark background. All you can see is my face atop a radiant red splotch.

Jane is amused. "You look like an M&M."

I do. I look like an M&M, bobbing in space.

Knowing this, I have no choice. I must tape the offensive photo to the wrinkled blue list of life directives adorning my fridge. Beneath it, I write my final instruction:

AND DON'T WEAR RED IN PHOTOS.

16 Thanksgiving

Imagine sitting at a long banquet table crammed with all the usual Thanksgiving goodies; the turkey and cranberry sauce and sausage stuffing and mashed potatoes and sweet potatoes and turnips and green beans and creamed onions and pumpkin pie and twelve other kinds of pie. Then imagine someone crashing in, leaping onto the table, stealing the turkey and bolting through a window, leaving a trail of drippings.

This would be a hair-raising interruption of your meal. The table, so carefully laid out, would be a shambles of upended earthenware. Your Uncle Tony would be wiping gravy off of your Cousin Martha's ponytail. Your Great Aunt Fanny would be blowing a gasket, maybe faking a heart attack. You would all mourn the intrusion, the disruption, the loss. But you would clean up. You would right the salad bowl. Straighten the dishes. Whip up some more potatoes. You would then sit down, put your napkins back on your laps, and continue eating. Because, even without the turkey, you would still be present at a feast.

This is my life post-Chris. It remains, despite everything, a bounty. I have so many causes for gratitude, chief among them my three children. At night, after saying prayers with Mitchell, he tells me I'm "greater than the greatest mom any boy could ever ask for," and I tell him the same is true for me: He's greater than the greatest boy any mom could ever ask for. Jeanne and Madeleine are greater than the greatest girls. Jeanne will soon be auditioning for *My Fair Lady*. Madeleine, full of gumption, plans to return to Ecuador the Saturday after Thanksgiving, just two months after she jetted home for her father's funeral. How blessed I am to be their mother. How blessed I am to hug them, to know that I'm hugging them with their father's arms as well. He can't, so I will.

My gratitude extends beyond them, to the boundless network that's hefted and shouldered us these first weeks. As Chris once said, "Amy, for someone whose family is dead, you have *a lot* of relatives," and that's never felt truer than it feels now. Everyone's a cause for thanksgiving—both a loved one at the table and a part of the feast itself. Everyone is a gift from God and someone else. The Ringwalds, all so tender and unflagging in their love, are abiding gifts from Chris. "You'll always be family," says his sister Anne, and I all but collapse with relief. The Richardson clan, blunt-talking and bursting with laughter: They're gifts from my mother, who met them through work.

My sister, Margaret, and her husband, Murray, are gifts from my late father and his first wife. Pam is a gift from the Richardsons: I met her through soccer, and it was Dan who first recruited me to play. Tamar and Sue are gifts from my sister Lucy: they were her best friends and roommates at Harvard. Jane and Bob and so many others are gifts from Chris: I married into my friendships with them, and so their laughter with him, love for him, pre-dates mine. Everyone in Albany is a gift from Chris, too: Had we not fallen in love, I wouldn't be here at all. I wouldn't be living in this neighborhood, on this street, answering this doorbell to find some caring friend with a tray of cookies. I wouldn't be scratching out Neil Young and Tin Pan Alley and Talking Heads on my fiddle in a living room stuffed with bandmates. I wouldn't be striding past the forty-seven other houses that crowd the block with mine, all but one identical: tall, narrow, modest 1920s homes with wet basements and occupants menschy and true.

I think of Mitchell's friends, who materialized after his father died and ran off to play baseball with him that first, abominable day. And Jeanne's friends, who sat in the kitchen

popping cheeseballs and laughing; they were racing to see who
could cram the most in their mouths at once. They're gifts.

The mailman who asks how I'm doing. The bank tellers and
managers, all of them so patient, who helped me set up the
children's social security accounts. The owner of the photo shop,
a kind Moroccan-Israeli who wrote me a note saying that in his
mind, Chris will always be striding past his store on a walk
through the neighborhood. They're gifts. Mr. Green, the Polish
tailor, who fled his village as the Nazis invaded and never saw
his parents again. He asks me how I am, gives me a look that
acknowledges so much more. It isn't necessary to say everything
to this man, who knows too much of loss. He nods. He knows.
He's a gift. The people who write us letters: they're gifts. The
people who bring us food: they're gifts. The people who pull me
into a hug and shove their lips to my ear and tell me they're
praying for us: they're gifts.

On Thanksgiving, we drive down to Westchester to join
Chris's family. His brother, Tom, and his wife, Paula, put on a
sumptuous spread. Tom lifts a toast to absent loved ones, and
we all eat and talk and laugh, somehow. His three boys, now
fine, funny men in their twenties, speak to me and the children
with a maturity and loving-kindness that breaks my heart. How
much time has passed. How grateful I feel for all of them, all of
these Ringwalds, whose love for my husband and children
reaches out to envelop me as well. I did nothing to earn it. All I
did was love a good man to the end of his life. And from that
love came more love, and more love, and more.

Thanksgiving night, we head to Brooklyn to visit our
friends, Vicki and Jim, and their kids: another four gifts from
Chris. He met Vicki during his year in graduate school. We eat
their leftovers and gab and walk and play games and make
music, Jim on banjo, I on fiddle. We busk outdoors for a while.
We talk about the lessons learned from Chris's life, the brevity
and strangeness of everyone's, and we agree there's no more
time to waste. We must live truly and fully and now.

Saturday night we say goodbye, pile into the Matrix and drive to the airport to send Madeleine back to Ecuador. Chris's oldest brother, Carl, and his wife, Karin, meet us there, and Madeleine's friend, Carissa. It's a hard goodbye. Madeleine doesn't want to leave, but she wants to finish her year abroad; someday, she wants to look back and see she did it. She knows the grief will follow her there. She knows she'll be homesick. But there, in the cold rush of an airport, we form a scrum around this daring girl. She squeezes us, she cries with us, she prays with us. We have a family hug and say the doggerel that goes with it. Then she breaks away and wades into the current of travelers, letting it carry her forward.

It takes faith, even a kind of lunacy, to see her go and know that I can't follow. That was hard enough when Chris lived — when we first saw her off for her year abroad, just a month and a half before he died. Watching her leave was difficult then, impossible now. I have no greater cause for thanksgiving than my three astonishing children, and I have no greater fear than failing to be there when they stumble. I can't trail Madeleine through the airport and onto the plane and into the air and over land and sea to Ecuador. She takes those steps without me. Without her brother and sister. Without Chris. How she does that, I can't fathom. She figures it out alone.

17 Not a Sad Tink

I am one lumpy dame.

Now, if women are being honest, they'll confess to feeling lumpy most of the time. The feminine ideal, up until the age of flappers and Twiggies and Tom Wolfe's astutely observed "boys with breasts," was curvy. Or so we're told. This, we observe when we see all those happy chubby cheeky ladies in Renaissance paintings. But when a man says "curvy" nowadays, what he really means is "chesty," or so most women believe, and most women don't have quite enough bosom-specific curves to classify as such. Instead, we have hip-specific curves, stomach-specific curves, thigh-specific curves, behind-the-knee-specific curves, gelatinous-stuff-squishing-out-between-the-bra-straps-specific curves and flappety-wapping-below-the-arm-specific curves that serve no purpose I can divine other than to make a woman feel like a large winged rodent. And this is not what a man means when he says "curvy."

No, most women don't feel curvaceous. We feel bumpy, chunky, and thick. The only good part about being and feeling this way is the fact that, for many of us, we find ourselves in this condition having given birth to one or more beautiful children. So our husbands tend to be down with it. Or if they aren't down with it, they don't say anything, or they won't be getting any, up or down, you feel me? For the same reason, they also tend not to complain about stretch marks, pregnancy scars, and distressed bellies that look like chichi designer handbags. And women, as a result, tend not to care.

Until their husbands die. Then they care. Then they begin to wonder if any man would ever want to have sex with them ever again, or at least, you know, not ralph up a cow at the sight of them naked; it's just as well that some of them plan on entering convents. The insecurities set in. The sense of lumpiness prevails.

In my case, the lumpiness extends to small, literal lumps: benign cysts that come and go, swelling and draining as the spirit and fluid move them. This is a recurring theme for me. It is, as recurring themes go, more of an annoyance than a serious health problem, but the annoyance can top out somewhere near paranoia when I happen to stumble across a fresh new thingy in the already thingy-laden zone known as my breasts.

My first response is always: SHIT! Another cyst! What a drag!

This is then followed quickly by my second response, which is: SHIT! Unless it's breast cancer! Then it's more than a drag!

And then my third response: NO, YOU MORON! IT'S ONLY A CYST! Just wait and see! It'll shrink on its own!

And then my fourth response: But it could still be cancer! Shit! I might be dying! I have to be sure! I have to get a mammo! Shit!

And finally, my fifth and most rational response: Fucking mammos. I *hate* those things.

When I find my latest mammalian nugget, the internal shouting match takes on an even more urgent tone. This time, I think immediately of the children. This time, I realize, I can't muck around and wait through a menstrual cycle or two until the hateful thing drains on its own. Because I can't risk it. Because the kids just lost their father, and I CAN'T DIE.

This is some shit I have to figure out, and fast. Enigmatic gazunga shit waits for no woman, even a woman with no one to hold her hand while she's coming unglued with anxiety. Especially her.

And so I call for an appointment with my gynecologist, who confirms the lump and tells me, yup, I need a mammogram and probably a biopsy, too. (At the word "biopsy" my brain howls: FUCK FUCK FUCK FUCK FUCK.) I then call for a mammo. I show up for the mammo. I slump in a drably carpeted room alongside other women awaiting mammos and a few quiet, supportive men, their forearms on their knees and their faces caught somewhere between love and boredom.

After too many minutes of this, I hear my name, and I look up. It's an ample woman with a clipboard. "You are Amy?" she asks in a rock-and-rolling Russian accent. "How are you today?"

Yes, I'm — or so I begin to reply. But she interrupts me.

"Of course, eeef you are here, you are not so good, yes?"

Uhhh, I begin to reply. But again, she interrupts me.

"Let us go and see."

And so she takes me to the dreaded inner sanctum of Mammo Central, that complex of rooms designed to give women every opportunity to feel like guest stars in the melodramatic season finale of a hospital drama. There, I remove my shirt and bra and shrug into a gown, tying it loosely at the front for easy access. Then I step out into the corridor, in search of my bluff Russian helper.

Hello? HELLO?

"There you are. In here," she instructs, and I am brought into a room with a hulking torture device intended for one purpose and one purpose only: to make me wish I were a man. In every other circumstance, I am content to be female. But having my boobs squished to the thickness of whole-wheat toast (i.e., one stop shy of Wonder Bread) and then jerked around at oblique angles has a temporarily deleterious effect on my gender identity.

The ample Russian sets me up at the vise, I mean garlic press, I mean mammogram machine. Which breast, she wants to know. Right, I tell her. What's the problem, she queries. A lump, I tell her.

"Oy," she says. "I hope is not a sad tink."

I could not agree with her more. I hope is not a sad tink, too.

"Let us see."

She takes my right breast, slaps it between the machine's two plates, then starts the important job of precision limb placement. Men might not realize this, but having one's knockers X-rayed requires the arduous manipulation of one's arms, hands, shoulders, and feet, on which one is sometimes forced to stand tip-toe while one's bosom is being tilted and twisted into exciting new shapes. One feels like a blob of pizza dough. It is so, so much fun. Good for your balance, too. Try it!

"Put your right arm here."

I put my right arm here.

"No, higher."

I put it higher.

"Higher."

Higher.

"Hold that."

I hold that.

"Now your left arm. . . *so*."

I put my left arm *so*.

"Down."

I put it down.

"Hold still."

I hold still. She cranks up my tit nice and flat. Tips it. Cranks it up more. If there is a sad tink somewhere inside, it is waving a tiny white flag of surrender.

"Wait," she says. "Is not good. I do it again."

And so she uncranks me, re-configures my boob, bosses around my arms some more, cranks me up again, and once more tilts my bosom akimbo. The skin on my chest is so tight it's on the verge of tearing. So this is obviously a good time for her to ask me about my lump. Did I find it myself?

Yes, yes, I say. I'm very cystic. I get lumps all the time. But my husband died in September (WHY do I say this?), and I want to be careful. For the children, you know.

She mutters a few vexed noises. Then she asks me how old he was, which everyone asks, and I tell her 55. She groans in dismay. Then she asks me how he died, which everyone also asks, and I tell her suicide. She groans even more loudly in even more dismay. "That is terrible. How terrible."

Yes, I agree. It is terrible.

"And now *dis*... " She nods at my smooshed right breast, then shakes her head. "So sad. So terrible for you."

Oh, how I love the Slavs. They do not minimize unhappiness. They do not sugar-coat misfortune. When something sucks the big one, it sucks the big one, and if the particular Slav happens to be Tchaikovsky, the unhappiness merits a booming orchestral tutti in a minor key. I need him right now to wheel a few timpani into the mammography room.

The ample Russian, having affirmed my torment and situated my boobs, steps away behind a lead screen to snap my photos—which, when they're finally read, reveal exactly what I thought they'd reveal. A cyst. Which prompts exactly what I thought it would prompt. A biopsy. Which flings me into a few days of nail-chewing apprehension as I wait for the results, which indicate exactly what I'd hoped they would indicate. Nothing. A benign cyst. Nothing. Not a sad tink at all: breast shit successfully F.O.'d.

18 Smaller

A shorter tree. A different corner. Fewer ornaments. On Christmas Eve: a different church. On Christmas morning: a different house.

There's no Chris this year, and no Madeleine, either. Jeanne and Mitchell and I know early on, long before the dawning crack of Advent, that this will be difficult. There's no way it can't be. A grief counselor warned me about the first year's milestones. The first *this* without Chris. The first *that* without Chris. Not that the seconds and thirds and fourths won't also hurt, but the firsts—like the lasts—pack a special wallop. They're a type of shit that cannot be diminished, avoided, or ignored. You can't turn your nose and step over them. Christmas is coming no matter what; it's going to suck no matter what; the F.S.O. task at hand is how best to endure its suckiness.

As the seasonal suck factor approaches with growing menace, its harbingers are twinkly and tinseled: the sleigh bells on the radio, the garland draping stores. After a week or two of this, I decide I want to strangle Bing Crosby. Good thing he's already dead.

So the children and I discuss our options. We can do what we usually do, but do it Dad-less and Madeleine-less: Get a big tree, throw a big party to decorate it, go to midnight Mass, wake up in Albany, then drive down to Connecticut for dinner with the Ringwalds at the warm and gracious home of Chris's sister, Anne, and her husband, Bobby.

No way can we do all that. Especially the big-tree-and-party part of the plan. No. Qualifier. Way. Instead, we head off to

Home Depot with Jane and Maxim, choose a scruffy little pine—
like that runt of the litter in *A Charlie Brown Christmas*—and toss
on a few shiny orbs from a box in the attic. Chris loved his
ornaments, and there are crates of the things up there. He loved
to raise the tree, always a tall and full and proud one, always in
the same living room corner each year, and he loved the ritual of
stringing the lights and positioning the angel and opening our
home to friends and neighbors.

I loved it, too. Maybe I'll love it again someday. Just not
now. For now, we stick our runty tree in another part of the
living room. No idea where the angel is, anyway. And we don't
even bother with the lights.

As for our usual midnight Mass, it's unimaginable—the
thought of joyously anticipating the birth of Christ in just the
church, with just the friends, in just the seats, where we kissed
my husband's casket goodbye three short months ago. I love that
parish. We attend it weekly, and their support since Chris's
death has been a remarkable, reassuring mix of the earthly and
the prayerful. Catholics are great at that: love without
sentimentality. But we need to be elsewhere on Christmas Eve.
We need to find anonymity, for that one holy night, in some
place where no one knows us and loves us and looks up from
their hymnal and thinks, "Oh dear God. How tragic."

In the end, we decide to drive down early to Connecticut
and attend midnight Mass there, with Anne and Bobby, and
then wake to presents under their tree. This feels like the best
solution, the only solution. The necessary one. Its sense of
rightness grows as we drive downstate and worship in the
shadows of an old Danbury church, then utter goodnights with
hugs and heartache and rise, Chris on our minds, to the fun of
Christmas morning. Sipping my coffee, watching my children
tear open their gifts, I'm as groggy and as joyful as I ever am. He
isn't here, but they are. That's something. That's a *huge*
something. That afternoon, with the full complement of
Ringwalds milling around us, we Skype with Madeleine in

Ecuador and walk around the house so she can send her love and say her Merry Christmases.

Such a strange thing to say, "Merry Christmas." And yet we say it. We say "I love you," too, and "I miss you," "I'm proud of you" and "I miss Dad," and again "I love you, I love you." We say everything we knew we'd say going in. We feel everything we knew we'd feel. We knew it was coming, this first Christmas. And so it has. And we get through it.

Loved ones still laugh. People still eat. Voices still ring. Christmas still happens. But Stranger. Sadder. Different.

Smaller.

19 Things I Can't Say to Your Face, Part II

Such a father you were. How you loved the kids, celebrated them, laughed with them, challenged them, inspired them to be better human beings. Madeleine, like you, grew up to be a swimmer and debater with the steel-trap mind of a natural lawyer. Jeanne became a dancer, a soccer player, a singer, a mimic from the start. Remember how the pipsqueak used to imitate us? She was two years old, three tops. "This is Daddy!" she'd cry, opening her mouth wide and tossing back her head. We were in stitches. And Mitchell, whose birth we greeted with tears of exultant disbelief: "A BOY!?!" We didn't know we made boys. He is so like you—so small, and strong, and good, with a head built for complicated thought. But I like to think he gets his speed from me. Can you feel his joy now, when he runs?

I visit our friend, Betty, in the nursing home, and she talks about you. She remembers that you left your job. She remembers how distressed you were. I am unsure how to tell her that you died, knowing that she lost her own husband in a fall from a roof—accidental, yes, but just as sudden, just as sad, leaving her with just as many kids to raise alone. Two girls and a boy, long gone from cancer. Danny was his name.

Francis was Betty's husband. Frank. So handsome he was. His incandescent grin shines from a photo she keeps by her TV, and he watches us while we chat.

"How he loved the kids," she tells me. "How they loved him."

He was a great dad, wasn't he? I ask.

"He was a wonderful father. He would come home from work, and the kids would come running. Not just ours. All the kids, from the whole neighborhood." I reach for his photo, bring it close to Betty.

What a good-looking man, I say.

"Oh! So good-looking."

You must miss him, I say. And Betty turns quiet, considering me.

"You have a handsome husband, too," she says.

Yes. Yes, I say, avoiding verbs.

"Chris is such a wonderful father."

Indeed. Yes.

"You two are made for each other."

Yes.

"Such a wonderful father," she repeats, and I'm so glad she knows this about you. I'm so glad she remembers.

Yes, I affirm again. Yes. Such a father. Such a man. I hit the jackpot when I found him, I say.

"How is he?"

I brood over this for a moment or two. I've been a coward, not telling Betty that you're dead. I should. I should honor her by treating her like a full human being who can handle the news. I should honor you by treating your death with honesty. But I'm not sure how she'll take it. I'm not sure she'll take it at all.

Betty, I say, holding her hand. Betty.

She stares.

Betty, Chris is dead.

She stares.

Betty, Chris is dead. He died, Betty. He killed himself.

She stares.

Betty. Did you hear me? Betty. Chris is dead. He died. He died.

She stares. I stop talking. She stares again.

"How is Chris?" she asks.

I wait a beat, then take a breath and say it:

He got a job.

(You, sweet man—you know this isn't a lie. You did get a job. You held it a week, and then you jumped.)

"Thank God he found work," Betty says. "Thank God."

And somehow I smile and say: Thank God.

20 In Which I Begin to Regard My Legs Anew

Most guys don't appreciate this, but women—straight women, anyway—are equipped with highly sensitive Man Radar. This Man Radar performs a multitude of important services, including:

- ❖ detection of a man's sexual orientation;
- ❖ probing a man's availability status;
- ❖ ascertaining a man's attraction, either spoken or unspoken, to the owner and operator of the Man Radar;
- ❖ ascertaining a man's attraction, either spoken or unspoken, to potential feminine rivals, even those who operate at a remote location;
- ❖ detection, sorting, and ranking of a man's desirable attributes, including looks and personality;
- ❖ detection of flirting.

I should also note that certain functions of the Man Radar have been known to shut down upon initiation of a successful long-term relationship. After falling in love with Chris, I failed to notice when other men were flirting with me; either they stopped flirting, or I stopped caring, or both. I also stopped taking note of a man's many subtle cues indicating his availability. And one more thing: I stopped taking note of his looks.

Chris was it for me. Throughout two decades of marriage I suffered from looks-blindness, an inability to gauge any man's sexual appeal on any meaningful level. We never fell out of love, and because we never fell out of love, I never regarded another man as desirable. At all. Occasionally, one might register on an aesthetic or dimensional plane (regular facial features, wide shoulders, that sort of thing), but in terms of how this information affected my animal nature, the gentleman in question might have been a statue in the Louvre.

Months after Chris's death, this looks-blindness continues. All operations of my Man Radar remain dormant. I am still incapable of ogling men because, from my standpoint, there is nothing for me to ogle. I am still planning my future life as a nun and still maintaining a pelt on my legs worthy of an Alaskan muskox. Therefore, I am still wearing pants to church.

Then, one day, I notice a man in an alarming way. Immediately after, I call Jane.

Jane! Jane! I don't know what's happened to me! The weirdest thing! I seem to be attracted to X!

Her response surprises me.

"Well, of course you're attracted to X," she says matter-of-factly. "Because X is really, really, really, REALLY attractive."

He is? I mean, four *reallys* worth? Are you serious? He's always been good-looking?

"You never noticed?!"

I never noticed.

"Oh. My. God," she says. Jane is the only person I know who says this phrase fully punctuated. She then explains that X has been a looker all along. I had no idea.

However this happened, X seems to have thrown a switch. In the weeks that follow, I catch myself regarding and admiring men in ways that I hadn't for decades. This is distracting: I must control the urge to stare with eyes unclouded. This is also guilt-inducing: It feels wrong, as though I'm somehow betraying my husband. How could I ever look at any man but Chris?

Then I recall a conversation we shared a few times with the kids. He always initiated it, and he always said: "You know, if anything happened to me, I'd want Mom to marry again. I'd want Mom to find someone new. I wouldn't want her to be alone." I would say the same about Dad. And we would both mean it, with all our hearts.

The reality is tougher than you'd think. In any living, breathing marriage, the two people involved must accept the fact that they'll be sleeping with no one else for the rest of their lives. That's an immense concession for any human being. But when the deal works, it works because they're still genuinely and exclusively attracted to one another—even after years of experiencing each other at their farting, burping, crotch-scratching, nose-picking, toe-cheese-rolling worst. This demands three things: a laser-like focus on your spouse's best qualities; a willful blindness to your spouse's worst qualities, at least while rolling around in a tangle of limbs; and an all-encompassing blindness to everyone else.

I didn't notice other men because I *couldn't* notice other men— because my capacity to notice them had been disabled by my love for, desire for, commitment to Chris. I was maritally, monogamously myopic, capable of seeing and wanting just that one man for more than twenty years. Now he's gone, and the myopia has lifted. I find that I'm a blinking hermit exposed to the sun after a lifetime spent in caves. And it is almost too much to process.

I call up Jane again.

Y, I say to her. You know Y?

And Jane says: "Oh. My. God."

In the middle of all these revelatory abecedarian moments, I have one more: Maybe the nun thing isn't for me. Maybe, just maybe, I might want to be with a man again. Not X or Y, but someone. Someday. In some situation I can't even begin to picture. But I realize, in a moment of earth-quaking, body-shaking, psyche-aligning sexual comprehension, that life is long, that I'm still young, that I'm damned lonely, that it could happen. I could get close to another man of unforeseen origin at some unforeseen place and unforeseen time.

Holy shit.

I shave my legs.

21 The Checkout Line Jollies, Part I

Every now and then, someone comes up to me weeping. Most do not. Take Joe: he doesn't. On the very first day, he arrived bearing candy. Every couple of hours he sidled up, shoved a Twix bar or a Kit-Kat into my fist, then eased back down the street without a word. Later in the week, he reappeared at the door with a smile. "I've come to tell you priest and rabbi jokes," he said, and then spent a solid twenty minutes in this sacred pursuit.

So, no, not everyone weeps. But enough do that I begin to wonder whether anyone will ever again look at me without feeling haunted — by Chris, or by me. Because I have become, against my will, a harbinger of death. Imagine this. Imagine being the one person in an entire community whose presence reminds everyone that shitty things can happen, and sometimes do. However I was known before (an ink-stained wretch; middling fiddler; harried mom), I am now known as the Lady Whose Husband Made the News That Night, Remember? Gone are the days when folks ran across me in some public place, burst into a grin and howled, "Ames! How are ya!" Now they approach with moist eyes and ask, "Amy...?"

I'm grateful for their concern, and for those who express it. I'd be lost without them. I know that I'm the epicenter of everyone else's grief, and I know how fortunate I am to be supported by them in mine. Truly, I could not ask for a more loving and generous community: If you think you live in a great neighborhood, I'm here to tell you it's nothing compared to this one. I have literally dozens of friends in walking distance. More.

And the only way *not* to bump into them is to not leave the house at all—or to leave it only after I've disguised myself in a latex peel-away mask *a la Mission: Impossible.* I suppose radical plastic surgery might be an option. Or crossing the street when I spot someone I know. I've done that more often than I care to admit. Sorry! Sorry! In a hurry! I yell out, hotfooting it as though pressed for time. I feel awfully guilty doing this, because I know I should be gracious to everyone who needs to connect with me; they need to know that *I* know that they care; and they need to be assured that I'm all right. But sometimes I'm exhausted. Sometimes, when I'm out and about, I just want to be out and about.

One afternoon, I head to the drug store to buy tampons and pads. I am not embarrassing anyone but myself in revealing this detail, which I mention only because I am amused by the irony of having to purchase such things when I find myself at the tail end, and what fabulous word choice, of my reproductive life. Hormonally, sexually, logistically, there is no further reason for my body to go through the hollow monthly motions of prepping eggs for the womb. Even if some random sperm were to come knocking at my door, and I were to introduce it cordially to my latest, hopeful, blushing ovum, nothing of interest would develop between them.

But today I have a need for sanitary items, and so I plan a stealth mission to the big-box pharmacy. I have no great desire to bump into anyone en route. So I park in the lot, not on the street. Inside, I make a beeline for the feminine products aisle, snap up my selections, toss them into the basket, then scoot down past the magazines to pick up a trashy gossip rag for Betty.

In the checkout line, I zone out, adopting the expressionless, doughy face of an annoyed peri-menopausal female with a basketful of maxipads. Yes, I am tired and moody, but there are other reasons for this state beyond the death of my husband. At the moment I am not Amy the Quietly Grieving. I am, instead,

Amy the Quietly Menstruating. My only hope is that no one will notice me.

That's when I hear it.

"Amy...Amy."

I turn around. It's my friend, Z. She is a sweetheart. Bumping into her always lifts my spirits. But today, seeing me in the checkout line with my *OK! Magazine* and my jumbo box of Tampax, she throws her arms around me and immediately commences weeping. I hug her back. We embrace for a long time, ignoring the attempts to ignore us by the three shoppers ahead of me, two shoppers behind, plus one cashier and a young, hovering manager. Crying continues for the duration of the scene, although not by me.

Finally, Z pulls back. She says something about being sorry for my loss. She asks something about my welfare, the kids' welfare, how we're holding up.

We're OK. This is awful, this is hard, I miss him like crazy, I tell her. But life pushes us forward. There's no other option.

This has become my mantra: Life only goes forward. I've noticed that of late. Call me when you hear anything different.

"I'm praying for you," Z says, still weeping, and I thank her, and I thank her, and I thank her again. I mean it. Another hug, and off she goes. I take a deep breath and return my face to its fixed feminine zone-out — grateful for Z, and for the reticence of strangers who pretend that I'm invisible, who resist the urge to turn and stare. Someday, I'll stop making people cry — I'll stop personifying something so sudden, crushing, and dark. But that's out of my control. That's not my shit to figure out. Time, and tampon runs, will take care of it without me.

22 We Three Rings

I need the guidebook. Where is it? It must be here somewhere! You know, that thick wedge of a tome listing everything every widow needs to sort through her grief, spruce up her psyche and, while she's at it, conform to all those weighty, if unspoken, societal expectations? That one. I can't find the fookin' thing. I know it's here somewhere. Grrrrrgh.

Oh, heck! I forgot! There isn't one! All I have to guide me, from now on, is the drift and druthers of my own personal needs. Which aren't all that reliable. The fact is, I am utterly discombobulated and unsure of what to do next, or when to do it, or even whether to do it. When should I refer to my husband as "my husband," and when should I refer to him as "my late husband"? When should I remove his name from the checks? How soon is too soon to attend a party? How should I respond when a stranger makes some passing comment that assumes I'm married? And what on earth should I do about Chris's Facebook page? Shut it down? Keep it up forever as a memorial? Talk about Figuring Shit Out.

The thorniest issue, for me, is determining how long to wear my rings. I knew what to do with Chris's ring: put it on a chain, hang it in my closet. After the wake, the funeral directors asked whether I wanted to have it buried with his ashes. No thanks, I said. I want that ring. I gave him that ring. I slipped that ring on his hand. That ring remained there for two decades, softening and molding to the shape of his finger. I plan to keep that ring for evermore, or at least until I give it to my son.

As for my own rings, I'll give them to my daughters someday: the slim gold wedding band, purchased from a shop off the Boston Common; and the engagement ring, its two small diamonds flanking a ruby. Chris bought it from a Manhattan jeweler named Bobby (not lying) Satin, and he presented it to me about a month after he'd popped the question while cross-country skiing in New Hampshire. It was, and I dare you to challenge me on this point, the best proposal ever: He released the binding on one ski, dropped to his knee, said, "Will you marry me?" and then, when I shrieked my affirmative, double checked, "Really?!?" Then apologized for not having a ring. As though I cared.

The ring came later, at a restaurant in Hudson, New York, where the lovebirds gazed ceaselessly, meltingly, into one another's eyes, and the gentleman told his affianced that she deserved something better than a diamond. "I decided you're a ruby," he said. "Because rubies are rarer."

This ring and its unembellished marital companion remain on my left hand. How long should they stay there? Six months? A year? Two years? Once again, I have nooooo idea. In the first couple of weeks or so it was a non-issue: I still felt married. Of course I wore them. But now, as the icky-sticky reality of life without Chris continues to gum up my world, it is hard to believe that I'm anything but alone. He is so not here. I am so not married.

I raise this issue with the grief counselor. What should I do about the rings? I ask her.

"That's a good question," she says. "What *should* you do about the rings?"

Beats me. How long should I wear them?

"That's a good question," she says. "How long *should* you wear them?"

I have this feeling that I'm expected to wear them for a year.

"Why a year?" she asks.

Why a year? I dunno. I guess I'm thinking of the *yahrzeit*, I tell her. You know, the Jewish tradition that marks the first year of mourning. There's just something about twelve months. It seems like the expected length of time. And I don't want to seem like I'm being disrespectful and failing to honor Chris's memory, especially with his family. I don't want to hurt people.

The grief counselor gives me a look of frank assessment. She's a smart lady.

"You know," she says. "You know, when you lose a spouse at a young age, you're dealing with the grief. You're dealing with the reality of being a single parent. And you're dealing with everyone else's idea of widowhood—and how widows should behave. But only you can know what you're going through. Only you can know what feels right."

What am I going through? Everything.

What feels right? Nothing.

Back in high school, I auditioned for a role in *The House of Bernarda Alba*, Federico García Lorca's incredibly depressing play about grieving women in Andalusia. The audition required me to pair off with another student for an improv, and we were told to act out a scene in a hospital as though awaiting news of a friend in a coma. All I did was stare at the ground and rub some dirt across the palm of my hand, but I made the drama teacher cry. She didn't give me a part, though. Instead I was assigned to run the sound effects with my mother and, even more exciting, appear onstage as an extra during a funeral scene. For this I wore a long black dress with a heavy black hooded cloak and stood with other similarly dressed girls, all of us clutching rosary beads and weeping. Afterwards, Dan went up to Mama and said, "Amy looks awful in black."

Such was my intro to mourning and widowhood. This black-on-black perception of things stuck with me for a dozen or so years until I became an actual mourner, and I then I realized that the grief of our popular imagining is not the same as the reality-based grief that manifests itself in so many kaleidoscopic and wacky forms. I hadn't realized, for instance, that it's possible to laugh at a wake until tinkly keyboard Muzak was piped into the funeral home gathering for my sister Lucy, a classical pianist who whipped off Brahms like nobody's business. The ironic merriment this caused was almost worth the injury to our ears. Almost. In truth I nearly wound up grabbing the mortician by the shoulders, screaming STOP THE MADNESS!! and then spraying bullets into the stereo with my Kalashnikov. There were no such moments that I can recall in The *House of Bernarda Alba*.

But the rings.

What to do? Keep them on my left hand? Move them to my right hand? That would require some adjustment in size, which I'd rather not make (to either the rings or my fingers). Online widows support groups where I occasionally lurk feature long discussion threads on matters of ringdom. Some widows still wear them after five years. Some take 'em off and stick 'em in a drawer. Some wear them on necklaces. Some have them melted them down with their spouse's ring into some significant new piece of jewelry. Once again the message is: Do What Feels Right.

I'm not sure What Feels Right. I'm not sure anything, from this point on, will ever Feel Right. But after a few more months of wrestling with this issue, I have determined What Feels Wrong: the rings. The precious metal on my left hand has assumed the weight of a lie, a gargantuan lie, and it presses and burns and mocks me. My husband is dead; I need to acknowledge that to myself and the world, just as I stood before the world and swapped vows and rings with Chris. To pretend otherwise is to diminish the gravity and eternity of this loss. *He's* not wearing the ring. *He's* not married any longer. There may not be a guidebook for clarification, but if you crack open the Gospels, you'll find that little tale of the Sadducees trying to trap Jesus on this point—remember that question about the wife who cranked through seven brothers? They want to know which bro would be her proper husband at the Resurrection, and Jesus' response is, basically: Get a real question, Sadducees! There *is* no marriage after death! This is me rolling my eyes!

So off they come, the rings. Onto a pretty gold chain they go. Sometimes I wear them around my neck. Sometimes I hang them in my closet, where they dangle and mingle with Chris's, the three of them clacking softly whenever I swing the door.

The weight on my hand has lifted, now. The lie is gone. In its place is a lightness, sad but not unbearable, that I sense with relief and reckon as a mercy. My hand feels naked, but at least it tells the truth.

23 Looking for Mr. Manly Pants, Part I

Back in late November, I purged my husband's winter clothes. On many levels, emotional, spiritual, and musculoskeletal, this was a pain in the ass. I hated it. But it felt necessary. It felt like a moral imperative, making sure that Chris's warm clothing got distributed to folks in need. I trucked heavy loads of his boots and long coats and down parkas and wool suits down to the Cathedral pantry, where they were welcomed with glad cries. I even remembered to ring up the dry cleaners and ask about items he'd stored over the summer—turned out there was quite a bit. I hauled that stuff over to the pantry, too.

Phew. Glad to get that over with.

But now it's a few months later, and Lent is here. What to give up? Nothing. I am terrible at giving things up. For years and years I gave up sweets, and for years and years I ate them anyway, then confessed as much to priests. Finally, I got a priest who suggested that maybe I blow at giving things up, although he didn't actually use the word "blow." He was much more civilized about it. He suggested that, instead, maybe I ought to take something on, something prayerful, or helpful, or otherwise positive.

I said: Really?

He said: Sure.

I said: You mean, I don't have to continue giving stuff up every Lent and then fail miserably at it and beat myself with a stick?

He said: I think, at this point, you should consider the possibility that maybe you're called to do something else.

Hurray! I am called to do something else! I can continue to gulp back seventy percent dark chocolate as the spirit moves me! And so this becomes the Lent of Lindt, which I consume guilt-free while giving away the rest of Chris's clothes.

Chris had many nice clothes. He was a bit of a fashion plate, although he would never have described himself that way. A dapper, conservative dresser (I think he wore jeans once in our 21-year association), he filled his closet and dresser with gorgeous suits and ties and shirts and pants and shoes and belts, and so on, and so on, and so on.

Over the course of several trips, and several weeks, I haul away his clothes to the pantry, where, again, they are welcomed with glad cries. This feels good. It's depressing as all hell, but it feels good in the sense that it feels right. In the sense that, when one is grieving, one still must do whatever small thing one can do to help one's fellow travelers. It hurts, but it's necessary. It's loss, but it's love.

I scan his nearly-empty closet. All that remains: some random cycling garb, a few pairs of suspenders, and a sampling of ties I'll be keeping for Mitchell. Plus my father's (by "father" I mean the original biological Louis, not adoptive Dan) old midnight-blue tuxedo. Plus one more thing of his that Chris had tailored to fit: A pair of vintage 1950s wool check pants.

I love these pants. I love them because I remember my Daddy wearing them. I love them because I remember Mama giving them to Chris after my father died. I love them because Chris then wore them, year after year, bringing them to Mr. Green, the Polish tailor, whenever they needed a fix. I love them because they're old-fashioned and pleated and commodious and big-butted and confidently, beautifully masculine in a way that modern pants are not. I love them because they aren't "skinny," or "fitted," or "distressed," or "straight-cut," or anything else that asexually fashionable clothing tends to be these days. I love them because they're Manly.

After two decades of marriage, I miss having an adult male around the house. Of course I miss the one in particular with a profound and lingering ache that I don't expect will ever fade entirely. But I am amazed to learn just how much I miss the full-grown masculine model in general. It's not the absence of muscles and the related help with jar lids that I miss so much; it's the absence of all that other stuff, the scent and scratch of an unshaved cheek, the sound of a resonant tenor in the kitchen on weekends. I even miss the stuff that used to annoy me, like the whiskers in the sink and the big clumping footsteps that woke me at sunrise whenever he left for tennis.

I miss the folding of the boxers. I miss the buying of the ties. I miss the sliding of the collar stays into button-down shirts. I miss the hanging of the pants.

I like men. I loved the one I had. I want another one, please — a new Mr. Manly Pants in a pair of pleated trousers.

24 F.S.O., Part II

Every marriage has its quirks. Every marriage also a division of labor. In our marriage, my husband took care of the yard, the garden, house repairs, and generally anything that involved sharp or heavy implements. Among the sharpest and heaviest is the lawnmower, which weighs between 100 and 150 pounds and is at least a zillion years old, possibly even dating back to pre-Cambrian times, when there weren't any lawns, so that's saying something. It's a reel push mower, and when I say "push," I mean "push"—no engine on it anywhere. Nothing but human power to roll it around the yard.

After Chris died, I would periodically notice that the grass on my lawn was suddenly and miraculously shorter, just as I would notice that the leaves had been suddenly and miraculously raked, or that the garbage cans had been suddenly and miraculously lugged to the curb, or that the snow on the sidewalk had been suddenly and miraculously shoveled. But now spring has sprung around me, and I resolve to start suddenly and miraculously mowing the yard by myself.

Front and back combined, the green space surrounding my home is about the size of a large cafeteria tray. It does not take much time or effort to cut the grass, unless, of course, one is forcibly shoving one's own weight in steel over bumpy weedy holey pockmarked turf. There are wheels on this lawnmower. I see them; I appreciate their hardy Newtonian mechanics; they do nothing for me. I may as well shoulder a beached whale across my yard.

So I gather all my mental and muscular faculties for the job. I give myself pep talks. I stretch. This amuses the children, who see me lunging on the grass, and howl: HA HA HA HA! MOM IS STRETCHING BEFORE SHE MOWS! HA HA HA HA HA!!

Then, grabbing the handles with both hands and a mighty heart, I give the thing a shove and run at top speed from the patio to the rear of the bike shed, a distance of thirty-eight feet that normally takes six seconds to cross without the additional burden of antique lawn tools. With the mower, it takes a little while longer, maybe six to eight weeks, as I must pause to hydrate, stretch some more and wipe away the sweat. Then it takes an additional six to eight weeks on the return trip to the patio. All in all, each individual attempt at lawn-mowing requires a two-year commitment.

You can see how this might begin to wear on one. Indeed, I have started fantasizing about power mowers. You might think widows would fantasize about other, more carnal things, and I'm not saying they don't, but if they did, you wouldn't hear it from me, at least not in the chapter devoted to lawn mowing. I confess this power-tool fantasy in a phone conversation with my brother, Danny, who listens as I describe my latest extreme-sports assault on the lawn and my crazy dreams of buying an electric mower. The yard's so small, it seems nuts to get a power mower, I tell him. But I can't do this any longer.

And then Danny says it. The Truth that will change my life forever. He says: "You know, Ames...the new ones are lighter."

New ones? What new ones? There are...new ones?

"The new reel mowers. They're much, much lighter."

They are? You mean they don't weigh as much as my house? This had never occurred to me before. That companies might still be making the damned things, and that the technology and efficiency might have improved some since pre-Cambrian times.

"God, no. The old ones are fucking lame-ass heavy. Get yourself a new one."

And then my brother, being gung-ho and meticulous in all things grabbing his attention, lectures me on the joys of the modern reel mower and — even better — tells me precisely which one to buy. I order it that very day. It arrives two days later. Thrilled, I hoist the box — Yay! It's only thirty-five pounds! I can do this! I have the power! — and open it in the back yard, assembling it in a jiffy.

How to put a lawn mower together is now among the Shit I have successfully Figured Out.

Then I take it for a spin. "Joy ride" is more like it. No doubt the neighbors see me running around the yard with it, front and back, laughing and singing and kicking up my heels and squealing WHHHEEEEEEEE while throwing blissful kisses at the sky, but no one complains or calls the police. They are good folk. So are the kids, who see me in the ecstatic throes of lawn-mowing and ask politely about the new machine.

Mitchell: You got a new lawn mower!

Mom: YESSSSSSSSSSSSSSSSSSSSSSSSSSSSSSSSSSSSSSSSSSSSS! Look at how light it is! Look at how fast I can mow the lawn! WWWWHHHEEEEEEEEEE!

Mitchell: Can I try?

Mom: No. Get away. It's all mine.

Jeanne: (*Drily*) Guess you won't have to stretch any longer.

Mom: WHEEEEEEEEEEEEEEEEEEEE!

Another small triumph in the Figuring Out of Shit: How to mow the lawn without losing half my weight in sweat.

Later, cleaning up after dinner, I reach for the Tupperware in the cabinet under the microwave and a feel a surge of amazement when nothing falls on my head. Go, go, go! F.S.O.!

25 Stink and Weeds

And what about the laundry? I can't bring myself to do it. Weeks after I've cleared out the bulk of Chris's clothes, there remains a lump of stinky socks and undershirts on the floor of his closet. It beckons. Even with the door closed, I can feel it. With the door open, I can smell it, although doing so requires me to get down on all fours and shove my face into its wrinkled cottony mass. After a while, to simplify matters, I select two of the ripest white v-necks and place them on my nightstand. Then, before going to sleep, I take a long sniff and say goodnight to Chris.

I realize this is kind of pathetic. No, not kind of: TOTALLY AND UMABIGUOUSLY pathetic. Having yielded every other part of my husband to the earth, ashes to ashes, dust to dust, I now savor the last remnants of his lingering bodily funk. Because I can't touch him, I must inhale his B.O. The shirts become a kind of holy relic to me, like St. Catherine's mummified head, or those delightful papal organs in that church near the Trevi fountain.

I didn't do this with my sister. I didn't do this with my parents. But I'm doing it now, and the grief counselor assures me that I'm not wacko.

Fun Fact of Widowhood: It makes you sentimental about rancid clothing! Yes!! It makes you sentimental about lots of things, weird things, things you hardly even noticed when your spouse was upright and walking, and the more mundane these things are—the smellier, the grungier, the commoner—the more soupy and sentimental you'll get.

Tossing out his toothbrushes takes great intestinal fortitude. His DNA is on them! His spit! How could I part with his exciting microorganisms! But out they go, in deference to hygiene, with a prayer and a minor crying jag. After my sister, Lucy, died and I was cleaning out her apartment, I fell in a heap at the sight of her blue fleece slippers—there was something so intimate and innocent about them. Nonetheless, I threw them out. Chuck.

With Chris, the violent rupture that ended our marriage is tougher to handle, the detritus tougher to chuck, because he and I shared and inhaled everything about each other. People joke about the marital yuck of finding dirty socks on the floor, but after a while, his disgusting laundry and my disgusting laundry were more or less indistinguishable. His stink became as familiar to me as mine. Somewhere in the first few years of marriage I didn't even smell it; it became obvious and important to me only after he died, and I had lost every other bit of him. "It's so personal—it's like his voice," Jane remarks after I describe my obsession with the odiferous undershirts.

This is a fitting analogy, because I can't delete his voicemails, either. I can't delete his emails. I can't comb through his inbox, his outbox, his standing desk in the guest room. I can't purge or organize his tools in the cellar. I can't dispose of his work gloves. I can't clean off his night table. I can't toss out any scraps of paper with his handwriting. I can't clear his dresser top, or the uppermost drawer with its eye drops and boot polish.

And I can't turn the page on his weekday missal.

He prayed silently from it each night, following the evening readings through the church year. I rarely joined him in this. He was more formal in his prayer life than I am, more at ease with the many ancient traditions of Catholicism—a faith I came to late, as a convert, just a couple of months before I met Chris. When my mother died, it was my husband, not I, who snatched up her missal and began to read from it daily.

Since he died, it has turned radioactive. I can't move the page from 1156-1157, Wednesday of the Seventeenth Week of

Ordinary Time, Years I and II. It's permanently stuck on Matthew 13:35-43, in which Jesus explains the parable of the weeds in the field. It's simple: The field is the world, the farmer is Jesus, the weeds are followers of evil, and the good seeds are "residents of the kingdom." The harvest is the end of the world, and when it comes, all those nasty weeds will be gathered up and torched. What Jesus describes is the ultimate clean-and-purge, a sweeping spiritual garbage haul for the End Times. It's a giant sorting. A mammoth figuring-out. No mention of dirty laundry, but otherwise, I can relate. Go, Go, Jesus! F.S.O.!

Looking at this radioactive prayer book one day (but still not touching it), I remember one more item I haven't taken care of, one more piece of shit I've yet to figure out: The weeds in Chris's gardens. I, the Black Thumb of Death, married a man with a green thumb. Someday I'll yank away the crabgrass and dandelions and give his tender blossoms breathing room. Someday I'll get rid of his work gloves, too. Maybe clear off his night table. Turn the page on his missal, even.

But launder his stinky v-necks? Check back in forty years.

26 Ecuador Stories, Part I: Arrival

Today we're in Ecuador. This is a true fact, though I'm not sure why. How did it happen? Somehow, for some reason, mere months after burying my husband, I have decided that the thing to do is visit Madeleine on her gap year. Of course! It's one of Elisabeth Kübler-Ross's five stages of grief: Denial, Anger, Bargaining, Depression, and Dragging Your Children to South America. Anyway, I'm doing them out of order (does ANYONE go through them sequentially?), or I am when I'm not ignoring them entirely or, even better, experiencing them all at once.

I do have an inkling why we're doing this. Three inklings, in fact. The first and most important inkling is that I'm desperate to see my eldest daughter. Skyping is fine (hurray for the Jetsons and their visionary gizmos), but it does not replace holding my actual girl with my actual arms. The second inkling has to do with Easter. The seasonal suck factor that accompanied our first Chris-less Christmas applies to our first Easter, which I need to figure out in short order. The usual procedure, which I can't wrap my head around, involves Vigil Mass on Saturday night, Ringwalds at our house on Sunday. Easter-egg hunt in the backyard. Ham. Mashed potatoes. Chocolate-and-peanut-butter buckeyes.

Nope. Not without Chris. Not yet. Obviously, the only other option is a trip to a developing country. (Take *that*, Easter!)

The third inkling is trickier to explain. Since Chris died, the shit most acutely and chronically in need of figuring out is us as a family: Who We Are, and What We Do, and How We Proceed Without Him. Aside from the traumatic downsizing from five to four, the kids and I have to get a handle on our reconfigured family dynamics. There's no Dad to leap into arguments with a firm hand, no Dad to organize people and plans and things, no Dad to lead us all into the unknown with dash and self-possession.

Recomposing ourselves without him is a challenge long and odd as I realize, bit by bit, that in figuring shit out—as I did with the Tupperware—I can choose to arrange things in a new way. My way. Our way. Whatever way makes us as happy as happy can be. So I find that I'm lax about chores, discipline, all of it. Haven't the kids been punished enough? Do they need more scutwork to do, burdens to carry, than the stuff they're already doing and bearing? I think not. I think, instead, that we need to get outta Albany—the rituals and psychic ruts that furrow our lives here—and flee to the south for a wild Andean excursion. And while we're at it, heal.

But how frightening it is, this striking into the unknown without him. He was always the energetic leader, the hatcher of plans who hoofed ahead on walks around an unfamiliar city, a guidebook in one hand, a map in the other, while the four of us skedaddled behind him. It was Chris who got us downhill skiing. Got us camping on Cape Cod. Started us hiking the Adirondack High Peaks when Mitchell was only three. Helped me past my fear of heights and roller coasters. Suggested cool family trips to Niagara Falls, Ottawa, Montreal; dragged me over to the Shatner building at McGill and ordered me inside, knowing his Trekkie wife was dying to check it out but too embarrassed to say so.

"Let's go to Europe," he said one day, and there we went. He led us into every church he could find, dozens of them, ancient and spired and spilling with art, between Brussels and London. We four skedaddled as usual. Every nave we entered, every waffle we ate on the street, was his idea.

He didn't just take us on adventures. He was one. I'm not a mousey thing by any stretch, but Chris had one of the largest personalities of anyone I've ever known, and I adapted to it. I became accustomed to pacing myself alongside him, shadowing his steps, and following his moves for decades. Dancing without him isn't easy, and at times I resist it. (Lead? Get real! That's not my role!) And yet, I recognize this as another necessary form of F.S.O. It's another bag I have to carry alone—except it happens to be a lot of bags, and I happen to be lugging them several thousand miles.

So I'm determined. I have to find a way to push my children forward, take them places, make them laugh. "We never go on any *real* vacations, like, relaxing vacations at resorts," Jeanne remarks. "Instead, we go on adventures."

Exactly. And this time, it'll be me who leads them.

Unless this is all a crock. You think? Could it be that I'm simply at a loss? That I've just cracked up? It's possible I'm still so flummoxed by my abrupt entree into single momdom that I've come unzipped. But hey, if I'm going to unzip all the way, frolicking pantslessly in some spazzariffic mono-parental breakdown, I may as well do so in the Ecuadorian cloud forest, yes? Yes. The way I see it, we have two choices: We either go as an act of strength and courage, hoping to remake ourselves in a land with no traces left by Chris, no memories of him, no signs; or we go because I'm a hopeless fucking basket case.

Either way, it makes sense.

Once this decision is made, a riot of further F.S.O. ensues. I figure out flight shit, itinerary shit, vaccinations-against-exotic-disease shit (yellow fever! fun times!), adapter shit, phone shit, currency shit (that shit's easy, as they take the American dollar), hotel shit and, lest we forget, shit shit (I heart charcoal pills). Then there's the killing-eight-hours-in-Miami-International-Airport shit.

Once in *Sudamerica*, the shit continues. After landing at Guyaquil Airport in the western coastal province of Guayas, we're greeted with whoops and hugs by a tanned and jubilant Madeleine, who rushes out from the crowd and all but tackles us. What a joy it is to see her. After introducing us to her family's driver, the soft-spoken Roberto, we pile our bags into a shiny Hyundai SUV and head for the beach town of Puerto Lopez, where Madeleine's host family is spending Easter weekend.

Here, at the point in the story that involves a three-hour drive to the Pacific, I must explain the scariest shit we encounter in Ecuador—scarier than the active volcanoes, the packs of dogs, and the forceful and copious throwup ejected into a gallon-size Zip-Loc by someone I shall not name in the Hyundai that first night. (Someday I would like this person to take care of me in my dotage and, I hope, wipe drool off my shirt when the situation demands.)

The holy terror is first introduced to us, unwittingly but persuasively, by Roberto, who is as considerate and quietly giving as every other Ecuadorian we meet over the next eight and a half days. He is also completely bonkers behind the wheel. And by "bonkers" I mean: He is obviously trying to get us annihilated! Yes!!! Why else would he drive directly into oncoming traffic? Why else would he charge down the wrong side of the street at 80 mph until scant microseconds before a tragic head-on collision, at which point he swerves abruptly in front of a bitsy pick-up truck carrying twelve men, six dogs and a goat? I am tempted to grab the wheel and yell STOP IT BEFORE YOU WASTE US ALL, ROBERTO, but do not, belatedly realizing that doing so would somehow disrupt Roberto's otherworldly Ecuadorian cool. He clearly believes he isn't going to die ("This won't kill me!"). This belief protects us.

In this manner—almost dying at high speeds, and yet somehow totally OK with that—we pass through one dusty town after another, pushing past packs of strays (the dogs, the goats, the pigs, the cows) as they traipse alongside us or munch on trash. Meanwhile, the Barfer barfs.

In the morning, when we awake at the beach, the world looks surreal in its brightness. We take a daytrip to an island with Blue Footed Boobies and snorkeling. I leap into the water from the roof of the boat; the kids snap a picture of my middle-aged ass mid-flight. Later, eating *ceviche* with plantain chips, I marvel at the country's rugged beauty—and at the newness, so simple and thrilling, of being with my children in a place so blessedly foreign.

Chris is more absent than he is at home, where he's always with us, always the unheard feet on the floorboards and the unfelt hug at the end of the day. Sometimes, back in Albany, I feel like a gap-toothed smile; people look at me and only see what's missing. In Ecuador, we move through space without his spectral presence, for he was never present here at all. Here, he never existed. Here, no one knows he ever *was*, and no one thinks to ask.

But we're here. We're still together. We're still loving and laughing and barfing and swimming, plunging through life and launching off boats into the azure Pacific. And I have an inkling we're happy.

27 Ecuador Stories, Part II: The Middle

Easter happens. We knew it would. And when it does, we miss it. We get the Vigil Mass time wrong at the church in Portoviejo and scramble inside just as the throng is preparing to leave. That's one way of coping! Skip Mass completely! So what if everyone gives us funny looks!

What a bad Catholic I am. Instead of going to church Easter morning, we stick to our original plan, which is to hit the beach again first thing. We borrow the Hyundai—that's me at the wheel this time, adopting the Ecuadorian driving philosophy and NEARLY KILLING US ALL—and visit San Clemente for sand and waves and more *ceviche*, then on to Crucita for dusk and a rapturous sunset. After that, Quito, where we bop around on a morning bus tour to visit the old city, the Plaza Grande, the presidential palace, the shimmering golden nave (our first as tourists without Chris) of the Compañía de Jesús church, and the 150-foot winged virgin attended by tourists and tchotchke salesmen. We share a long, yummy lunch with Luis, a gracious friend of Bob's (he of the HAHAHAHAHAHA's) who owns a restaurant so high on a hill above downtown that it might lift off and fly, and we ride a *Teleferico* cable car up a volcano shrouded in mist. Chris isn't with us then, and he isn't with us later as we head back down, plunging through the same thick fog and laughing.

There, hunched inside a funicular as it slings through the clouds toward Quito, I regard my kids with love and a strange, sad wonder, remembering what my dad said in the kitchen that first day. He was right; my life isn't over, and my life is more than the kids. But as they sit, all squished together on a bench seat opposite me, bouncing and joshing and mugging for photos in the mists of Pichincha, I know that their lives are complete with each other. *They* are a family unto themselves. I'm part of that family now, and I pray to God that I will be for decades. But they're the heart of it. They're the soul of it. Without even trying, they've figured that out on their own.

The next morning, we visit the *Mitad del Mundo*: the middle of the world. It lies north of Quito, which is the wrong direction for us—later we'll be heading south, to Baños de Agua Santa— but if you come home from Ecuador without visiting the equator, your friends will think there's something wrong with you. If the yellow stripe that splits the *Mitad* delineates something besides the actual, factual, latitudinal belly strap around the planet's midriff, who cares? Not us. We don't give a fig about modern cartography or the notable geopositional data shift since the middle's first marking in the mid-1700s. It's still there, and it still matters, and it still feels like the center of things.

The metaphoric punch of the place isn't lost on me. It's a sunny day but not quite warm, and I'm not quite cheerful— we're all grumpy and hungry, as breakfast didn't stick to our ribs—but we wander around the wide stone boulevards and circle the chunky obelisk, craning our necks at its base. I already have a headache. This isn't helping. But each of us dutifully straddles the line, one foot here, one foot there, smiling for the camera from a stance in two worlds.

And suddenly I see it. In this place, at this figurative division between north and south, I see the *mitad* marking two clear hemispheres in my own life. The rift occurred in that one savage, distended moment when I heard the doorbell, saw the cops, answered their questions, asked my own (did he jump? is he dead? what should I do now?) and felt everything I knew shear away from me. That was my demarcation, my zero-degree parallel between here and there, before and after. I'm now bisected. I see a world on either side. The equator splitting them, like this simple band of paint beneath my feet, doesn't agree with any standard GPS that calculates our lives in years. Unless I make it to ninety-six, the halves of my life are not exact. But they're unmistakable. They're unyielding. There is no crossing over, no foot on either side, no straddling between them for a picture. No going back.

This is my life now, my family now. This is how we move and live and love and have adventures — no longer skedaddling behind the daddy, but scurrying along together, side by side. Yesterday we were scrunched inside a cable car. Today we're bickering and stamping around a monolith like hypoglycemic pagans. And tomorrow? Will it be bickering and stamping again, or something else? Some yet-unseen source of excitement or nausea? Whatever it is, we're doing it, we're living it, we're pushing ahead, we're there.

We hit the bathrooms, then tumble into the car and travel south, toward the Amazon.

Adventure awaits.

28 Ecuador Stories, Part III: Whitewater

And so we've arrived in Baños, a town nestled along the edge of the cloud forest at the base of Tungurahua, another active volcano with another shrouded maw.

We've barely checked into our hotel when the kids start planning for an action-packed stay. We walk to a small block downtown that's loaded with storefront expedition businesses— little places where one or two people, generally a sweet tiny lady and an impossibly beautiful baby, sell afternoons and days doing all sorts of exciting things in and near Baños.

One catches our eye. Out front is a poster full of smiling people engaged in various adrenaline-pumped activities: canyoning, bungee jumping, rafting, other hair-raising and potentially lethal forms of recreation. We dutifully study it and even more dutifully argue about it. We are, at this and many other moments during our trip, the loudest people in Ecuador. The cacophony attracts the notice of the sweet tiny lady, who emerges with her impossibly beautiful baby and discusses the options with Madeleine.

I know that I'm relying more and more on this capable, gutsy daughter of mine—leaning on her skills as translator, cultural liaison, parental proxy—and I know that I probably shouldn't. But I have neither the fluency nor the deal-making skills to haggle a price with an Ecuadorian merchant, and so I let her dicker away, *muy rapido*. The upshot: rafting the next morning and horseback riding in the afternoon, for $35 a head.

The sweet tiny lady explains where we should be and when, what we should bring for the rafting (sunblock, swim suit) and the riding (long pants, a sweater) and assures us that the horses' route through Baños is along lightly trafficked streets. I'm glad to hear this because, once again, the prevailing philosophy on Ecuadorian roads seems to be: "This won't kill me." (As in: "I am now passing five cars on a blind curve up a narrow mountain pass with a cliff on one side and a wall of igneous rock on the other. This won't kill me.")

The next morning we show up, climb into a couple vans with Ecuadorian and Dutch tourists and tool along stunning mountain roads to the Rio Pastaza, where we squeeze into wetsuits and shrug into life jackets and adjust the flimsy plastic helmets being passed around. Our guide—a tall, droll man with enough forceful English to get and keep our attention—runs through the safety measures, which boil down to: This is the rope. Grab the rope if you think you're going to fall in. If you do fall in, grab the rope on your way down. If you don't grab the rope on your way down, be extra sure to grab it on your way up. Most of all: Don't fall in! Because falling in really sucks! We don't like it when people fall in!

OK, so he doesn't actually say: falling in really sucks! (He does, however, actually say: We don't like it when people fall in!) Nor does he say: By the way, you're about to enter Class 4 Whitewater, and you could die! Ha ha ha! No one tells us that. No one makes us sign a waiver that says, "I acknowledge this is a dangerous activity, and it's not anyone's fault but mine if I and/or my children are grievously injured and/or lose our shoes or worse." They keep this information on hold until the end. Were someone to explain everything at the outset, I might think twice about getting into the raft with my three angelic children. I might say SCREW THIS ADVENTURE and then skedaddle us all away.

The guide reassures us he'll keep Mitchell safe. Good. I thank him for that. Nice man. So we climb in and hoist our paddles and, resting our butts on the edge of the raft, huff and puff down the river, which very quickly becomes a raging river, which very quickly turns into foaming, crashing rapids. I think, Oh no Oh no Oh no. "Forward!" yells the guide. "Reverse!" yells the guide. "Stop!" yells the guide. And so on, as monstrous waves engulf and tip the boat. I think: My children must not under any circumstances fall in, because that would really suck.

Mitchell sits opposite me. He's having fun. The girls sit in front of me. One is having fun, the other is decidedly not (that would be Jeanne). I am having fun. I think: This is thrilling! Then I think: I am scared shitless! Then I think: But it's still thrilling! I'm really doing it! Maybe I'll do it again someday! Ha ha ha! The guide says, "Mami." I look over at him. "You like this?" Yes, I confirm. "It's not easy." No, but I like hard things, I tell him with some kind of idiotic and delusional middle-aged-lady pride. Then I think: What the hell am I saying! I am scared shitless! My children better not fall in! Ha ha ha!

During one wave, Jeanne whacks her hand on the paddle, cries out in pain and begins to panic. The guide pulls her over to sit next to him in the rear. I look back, worried. "Mami," he says, "keep paddling. I have her."

More waves. More thrills. More scares. Then, with a cool detachment that seems like fate in hindsight , an extra-super-big wave hits the raft and tips it on its heiny. I begin to fall back. I do not grab the rope. I continue to fall back. I still do not grab the rope. I try to persuade stomach muscles sadly attenuated by age and pregnancies to yank me back up, but they refuse. I fall in, and by that point, the rope is a moot issue. Later, the guide tells me I was underwater for all of five seconds. In those five seconds I had time to figure out the following shit:

Wow, I fell out. This really sucks. Will I drown? What if I smash into a rock? Am I going to die? The kids are probably freaking out. Better hold my breath. Better swim up and find air. What's that I feel above me? An object of some kind. Does that mean I'll die? Hmm. I'm not panicking. That's really weird. Oh, good, the object is gone. I can swim up now. Wait, another huge wave is crashing above—I can feel it—so I'd better not push up now, because if I do, I'll fill my lungs with water and drown for reallz. Just wait until it's passed. Dum-de-dum, dum, la la la. OK, time to swim up. Oh, goody! Air!

I breathe. And I yell out: I'm OK! I'm OK! I'm OK!

Jeanne holds out a paddle for me to grab, bless her. She and Mitchell and Madeleine are screaming in terror. I don't blame them. Again I say: I'm OK! I'm OK! I'm OK!

I grab the rope — better late than never — and tumble into the raft, gulping air. I'm OK! I'm OK! And then, impossibly, incongruously, I laugh. Later the kids tell me how scared they were when one purple flip-flop floated to the surface without me. Later they tell me a second raft passed over the spot where I fell in (the object I felt above me). Later I notice the cut on my knee and the small gash on my forehead; the paddle must have smacked me on my way down.

But right now I'm nothing but grateful, and so I laugh. I'm glad I was the one who fell in and not the kids. I'm glad I'm alive. I'm glad my capacity for F.S.O. extends to maintaining calm while getting tossed like jetsam in the whorls of the raging Pastaza. Here's something to figure out: how *not* to freak out when you realize you're submerged and you shouldn't swim up, because if you swim up, you'll drown. And you can't drown. You can't. Because your husband's dead, and your children need you, and fuck it, there is no option. Thank God I figured that out. Thank God, I say aloud. Once again I place my butt on the side of the raft and hoist the paddle, ready to go, plunging forward into our next great adventure. What was it I sensed in the cable car, and again at the *Mitad*? A new mode of being for our family, a new life and a new world for all of us? No going back? Well, then. Onward.

This won't kill me. This won't kill me. It doesn't.

29 Ecuador Stories, Part IV: Shit

In downtown Baños sits a basilica, the Church of the Virgin of the Holy Water (Nuestra Señora de Agua Santa), blunt and dark on the outside, vibrant and colorful within. The artworks on its walls go beyond the standard-issue Bible stories to depict a series of wild Baños miracles, most notably the tale of a man who fell from a snapped rope while traversing a crevasse. Mid-fall, he cried out, *"¡Madre mía de Agua Santa!"* and was caught by an unseen hand. The painting shows him dangling against a backdrop of clouds and jagged cliff faces, his round black hat winging like a Frisbee through the sky. Meanwhile, his virginal guardian levitates on a throne behind and above him. Quite a picture.

We visited that church first thing, partly from a sense of duty: It's famous, and we're here, and Chris would have brought us first thing, too. We didn't spend much time there—only long enough to say we did. But that one painting of that one story has followed me everywhere, ever since. The man flailing. The chasmal depth. The flying hat. The cry for help followed by the hand of salvation. Impossible not to think of that man as I dry off from my impromptu dip in whitewater. Impossible not to think of another man, on another descent much closer to home. And now, here, me. So much of life is falling. From the moment of crowning at birth to the lowering of ashes, gravity does its work.

But I survived. And because I survived, I have to confess that almost drowning was sort of a blast. Really and truly. No *way* could I possibly top that in my single-minded pursuit of buzzy family experiences. Follow me, children! Watch me lead! Hear me laugh in the face of death!

Or, in this case, shit. Literal shit; nothing woozy or fanciful about it this time. This time, our riotously entertaining adventure takes us straight up the butt of a large land animal.

Upon our return from rafting, we head back to the hotel, where I slather Bacitracin on my wounds while the girls and I discuss whether to wear long pants for horseback riding. I tell them they should, as the sweet tiny lady was awfully explicit about it in her instructions. She even wrote it down for us: LONG PANTS. Madeleine and Jeanne beg to differ. They are already wearing teensy-weensy shorts. I suggest they wear something more expansive. We find this an excellent opportunity to have another argument.

Madeleine: Mom. No. Listen. I am not going to wear long pants. Seriously. Mom.

Mom: But but but but. The lady said we should.

Jeanne: I'm not, either!!

Mom: But but but but. The lady said we should. There must be some REALLY GOOD REASON she said we should. There must be some REALLY BIG ISSUE for tourists wearing shorts.

Madeleine: Mom. Listen. No. I am not wearing long pants. I am not going to ruin them. Mom.

Mom: But but but but. You'd rather ruin your legs?

I actually win this argument. At 4 p.m. we appear once again at the storefront and the sweet tiny lady calls a taxi, which brings us five or six blocks to a yard with two men—one young, one old—and five smallish horses with pretty coats and banana-yellow flaps covering their backsides. With some aid we climb onto the horses' backs. The old man hands us the reins. His instructions: "Hold. *Un mano.* Left—go left. Right—go right. Up—stop." And we set off with the young man as our guide, winding slowly along the streets of Baños toward the Rio Ulba and the breathtaking mountains behind it.

The kids take to riding immediately. Mitchell's grin never leaves his face. "I LOVE horses, I LOVE horseback riding, this is so much FUN," he says throughout the ride, and the remainder of the day, and the days that follow. He and his sisters are utterly at ease. Madeleine's horse, Maria, is the leader. She is also the eater, stopping every few minutes to sample the grass while Madeleine laughs. Jeanne's is the biter: She keeps taking snaps at the other horses' asses.

Mine is the crapper. I can't see it, but the children inform me that his output is frequent, fluid, projectile, and green, and thus we grasp the reason for the banana-yellow butt-flaps. When the horses bump into one another other, smearing each other's fecal matter front, side, and tuckus, we also grasp the reason for the long pants. Shorts = horseshit on legs. Without saying I told you so to the girls, I say I told you so to the girls. Or maybe I really do say I told you so to the girls, more or less every time the fulsomely excreting ass of the horse beneath me shoots yet another fountain of equine feculence in their direction. And I love how florid one can be in describing manure, don't you? Regardless: PLEASE TAKE NOTE, FRIEND-OS, BECAUSE MOM-O WAS RIGHT-O.

Meanwhile, Mom's horse picks up speed at random intervals, causing her to bounce dangerously and painfully in the saddle. Mom is reminded that she almost fell off a horse at age 14. This reminder becomes especially pronounced when a pack of stray dogs emerges from the brush, coming after us with horrible growls and slavering fangs and dreadful purpose. The kids yell: Mom! Don't fall off! Don't fall off! Mom says: I won't fall off! I won't fall off! Meanwhile, Mom is thinking: How many more adventures can I take? For crap's sake, haven't I fallen enough today? Mom is also thinking: Screw you, gravity! Which is one stop short of an appeal to the *Agua Santa*. Mom has no idea what she's doing, but she yanks the reins up as directed ("Up—stop"), which the horse ignores, probably because the horse senses that Mom has no idea what she's doing.

In this manner we make our way down to one of the main thoroughfares that zoom past Baños, and I wonder about the sweet tiny lady's assurances that the horseback riding would only travel lightly trafficked streets. This is not a lightly trafficked street. This is a narrow but speedy two-lane highway with cars, buses and overloaded trucks screaming past, and I am again reminded of the prevailing Ecuadorian driving philosophy. (E.g., "I am now passing three cars and five people on horseback with oncoming traffic heading toward me at 100 kilometers per hour. This won't kill me.")

"*Derech'*, *derech'*!" ("Right! Right!") yells our guide, a slim, gentle fellow named Fabian, and we all do our best to comply. The kids and their horses are *derech'* enough for safety, thank God, but my horse veers ever farther into traffic. Horns blare. Engines gun. I yank on the reins. Again the animal ignores me. I think: Why does this horse hate me so? Does he smell my fear? He thinks: Would that stupid lady just leave me the #$%!?! alone? If only I could shit on *her* legs!

Without any instruction from us or Fabian, the horses wander off the highway and up a dirt trail that climbs to a picturesque waterfall—one of many beautiful *cascadas* in the region. The views are, like so many in this country, absolutely stunning. *Su país es muy hermoso*, I tell Fabian: Your country is very beautiful. We get off, watch the horses poop, snap photos, watch the horses poop some more, hear them fart, get back on, head back onto the highway and back past the pack of strays. This time, our horses start running before they appear. We do not fall off. We are not bitten by potentially rabid dogs. Not so far.

The next day, our last in Baños, heading off on a short hike for a better view of Tungurahua, we cross a bridge over a yawning cleft in the earth—perhaps that very same crevasse depicted in the painting of the hatless man. A sweet tiny lady *sans* infant sits at the midpoint with a bundle of cords and a pile of shiny buckled things, selling a la carte bungee-jumps into the abyss. The set-up looks a little sketchy, and I am not about to attach myself to a long rubber line and chuck myself over the edge. I'm not chucking my children over, either.

And yet the dizzying height fascinates me. All heights fascinate me now. There's no emptiness to them any longer; when they aren't filled with grief, they're filled with questions. I look down and think of Chris, what he felt and thought and feared, and I find myself meditating on miracles and failures. I had prayed for a miracle for Chris, just as I had prayed for a miracle for Lucy, just as all believers pray for miracles for their desperately suffering husbands and sisters. After Lucy's suicide, I spent some time dwelling on this pissiest of all religious conundra (why does God say "no"? why do I ask, and why do I still believe?), but after Chris's I didn't even bother. I know myself well enough by now to know I'll always believe, I'll always ask.

And sometimes, the Almighty replies in the affirmative. Jeanne's dream was as quick and vigorous a prayer response as any I've ever received. It wasn't just a "Yes." It was a "Yes Indeedy, Here You Go, And Would You Like Fries With That?"

So it happens. God nods. Men fall from great heights and live, whether cradled by luck or a hovering virgin. It's just that mine didn't.

30 Ecuador Stories, Part V: Monkeys, More Monkeys, and a Dog

In the midst of all these exploits, I keep sensing a Chris-shaped hole beside me — where he should be, would be, if he hadn't died. But of course if he hadn't died, I wouldn't have brought Jeanne and Mitchell to visit Madeleine in South America. Therefore, any attempt to envision him here, splashing paddles into the Pastaza or getting shat on by horses, is an exercise in futility, and a painful one at that. But I envision him. I'm human. I ask what he might have done differently, whether he would have marched us off in some opposite direction, ushered us into yet more churches or devised some other death-defying escapades sold on the street by tiny ladies.

There's no answer, and how could there be? These are our experiences, not his. And at a certain point in the midst of them — somewhere between the rafting and the riding — I stopped thinking quite so much about the Chris-shaped cut-out and started feeling, at long last, transformed. Just a little bit. Just enough to believe that I can lead; that I can travel and traipse without him; that my kids and I can, indeed, have our slam-bang adventures without him, be it here amid the staggering beauties of Ecuador, or anywhere else on the globe. We can keep living and racking up stories, I'm sure of that now. I'm doubly sure that he wants us to.

But I can't blame him for the monkeys.

Now, some people find them cute. Others find them disturbing and scary. I had always found them cute, and part of me (the stubborn, childish, idealistic part) still does, but after this trip's lesson in simian-related F.S.O. I also find them enormously disturbing and extremely scary. They are unpredictable, fast-moving, thieving little buggers.

This we learn during our stay in Puyo, a gritty jungle town about an hour from Baños. If you have only a day and a half left to visit the Amazon basin, Puyo's your best bet, and the drive south is—what's that word again?—breathtaking. More mountains. More clouds. More waterfalls: At the taxi driver's suggestion, we stop and hike up to the thundering *Pailón del Diablo* (Cauldron of the Devil), whose elemental force reminds me of Angel Falls at Niagara.

Once in Puyo, we take a cab to a jungle nature preserve where a guide takes us around and explains for us some of the endangered, exquisitely beautiful Amazonian flora. He hands us cinnamon leaves to chew. To the kids he hands a lip-shaped blossom; they pop it in their mouths and pose coyly for photos. On our return to the hotel, Madeleine asks the receptionist about fun things to do the next day. The advice comes back: Go see the monkeys in the jungle at the edge of town. Monkeys! Cool! Monkeys are soooo cute! Monkeys are fun! Yeah, all right, we're in the Amazon, baby! Monkeys!

So the next morning we take a cab to the *Paseo de los Monos*, a monkey rescue staffed by tall young Germans in khaki. A sign warns us to hang onto our stuff for dear life, because, for our information, monkeys are unpredictable, fast-moving, thieving little buggers. The sick, injured, and dangerous monkeys are all in cages, but the rest of them are not. They gambol around the grounds, perfectly at ease in the presence of humans. Some of them are wild monkeys who drop in for a bit of schmoozing at the primate happy hour and then return to their digs in the jungle.

We are all delighted. We are all charmed. Except for Jeanne, who is already among the group of people who find monkeys disturbing and scary. (Why I decided to exacerbate her fears with a visit to monkey headquarters mystifies me, now. Bad mom.) I am especially delighted and charmed when a curious Woolly monkey takes an interest in me and comes up close.

Mom: Look at that! He's so cute!

Mitchell: He's so cute!

Madeleine: He's so cute!

Jeanne: I hate monkeys.

Then the curious Woolly monkey comes up closer. Quickly. Straight to my feet. He grabs onto the bottom of my crop pants. Isn't he sweet.

Mom: Look at that! He's so cute!

Mitchell: He's so cute!

Madeleine: He's so cute!

Jeanne: I hate monkeys.

Then he climbs up my thigh. Then he climbs onto my back. Then he climbs onto my shoulder, hops onto my backpack and starts applying himself—with considerable speed and admirable monkey-industry—to the zippers. It appears the thieving little bugger is hell-bent on raiding my pack.

Mom: Ahhh! Get off me! Get off me!!

Mitchell: Ahhhh!

Madeleine: Ahhhh!

Jeanne: I hate monkeys.

Somehow, I shake him off. One of the tall young Germans materializes beside me with an undisguised look of disdain. "We tell everyone to leave their bags in the car," he says. Why, thank you for that helpful and timely piece of information, Herr Professor Doktor. Out loud I say: We took a cab. The tall young German shrugs in reply. I tighten the straps on my backpack, and the kids and I head down toward the river. A monkey begins to circle Madeleine, who quickly removes the cross from her neck and shoves it in her pocket.

Like everything else in Ecuador, this is all spectacularly beautiful. Cicadas chatter. A zillion types of palm trees soar and sway. A small, squat mammal with a long striped snout follows us around—it looks like a cross between an aardvark and a mole. And look over there! Another curious monkey! What a lovely surprise! This one is smaller, skinnier, light brown. A capuchin, I think. He approaches with a gleam in his eye, the thieving little bugger. And runs straight at me.

No way, monkey boy. This means war.

Immediately he mounts my leg and starts to climb. But I'm tougher than he is. I'm faster. I'm a tired but determined old lady, and I've learned my lesson from Monkey 1. I will go in with my superior something-or-other (uhh, size? intellect? sense of foreboding?) and strike without mercy. In other words, I will once more scream: AHHHHHHHHHH, GET OFF ME, MONKEY, AHHHHHHHHHHH! I will then shake him off at the knee and backtrack quickly, and he will skitter away into the jungle, demoralized and defeated.

The kids and I check out the river for a little longer, then visit the sick and injured monkeys while the big-nosed Aard-mole-thing follows us around. When we decide we've seen enough, one of the tall young Germans calls us a cab, and we head back to Puyo, where we suck down *batidos* (delicious fruity milkshakes) and pack up our stuff for the eight-hour drive through the mountains to Guayaquil for our flights home.

This was one piece of S I needed help in F'ing O: Who would take us over the Andes. Thank goodness for my old friend, Jim (the one I exploited that first night I flirted with Chris), who knows Ecuador well and has secured a man named Washington after a couple of other drivers fell through. We're sitting in the lobby waiting for him, snacking on blob-shaped pastries and bored out of our heads, when the last blast of shit hurls forthwith in my direction. Fittingly, this occurs when I get up and head for the bathroom.

That's when it appears: a big, barking German Shepherd. Apparently, he's been locked in a back room. Apparently, someone let him out by accident. Apparently, he sees me, smells me, senses me on some visceral canine level, and apparently, he hates my guts. Or at least he hates my right thigh, because he bounds straight for my leg and chomps down, hard. A rough translation of my response:

AYYYYYYAAAARRRRRGHHHHHEEEEEEEEEEEEEEEEEE EEEEEEOOOOOOOOOWWWWWWWWWWW!!!

A rough translation of the children's response: MOOOOOOOOOOOOOOOOOOOOOOOOOOOOOOOOOOOOOO OOOOOOOOOOOOOOOMMMMMMMMMMMMMMMMMMM MM!!!

Still screaming, I bolt into the bathroom and yank down my pants, examining the damage: long, bleeding scrapes and teeth marks, but no obvious puncture wounds that I can see. The fangs didn't cut through my pants. Nevertheless, I bleat for a few seconds in pain and abject fear (something more along the lines of WAAAAAAAAAAAHHHHEEEEEEEOOOOOH) while picturing myself being medivac'd out of Puyo for a rabies shot to the belly. Then I squirt Bacitracin all over the wound and cover it with band-aids. As I do, Madeleine and Jeanne blast into the ladies room, terrified.

Madeleine: I told them to call an ambulance! You could have rabies!

Mom: This isn't happening! This isn't happening!

Jeanne: You have rabies?!?!! Mom! Noooo!

Mom (*calming down, sort of*): Look, maybe the dog was vaccinated. And there aren't any puncture wounds. So maybe saliva didn't get through.

Madeleine: But maybe it did! And we don't know if it's vaccinated! We can't take that chance! THEY'RE CALLING AN AMBULANCE!!

In truth, they are not calling an ambulance. This has been deemed a non-emergency by the owner (of the hotel, and of the dog), who dispassionately enters the ladies room with a cigarette and begins to speak as though it's THE most normal thing in the world for her dog to attack hotel guests in the thigh. There I stand with my pants around my knees, shaking. And there she stands, a thin, blonde, 70ish woman with excellent English, telling me "It's OK, he's a good dog" between leisurely drags on her cigarette. She says it again: "He's a good dog."

To which I would very much like to respond, in either English or Spanish: HE'S A GOOD DOG, HUH? THEN WHY THE FUCK DID HE BITE ME IN THE LEG? But I don't say that. Instead I say, with a baffled shake of the head: ...*¿Porque?...* Why? Why did this happen? Why should your darling German Shepherd suddenly feel compelled to snack on my quads? To this she says nothing. Instead she takes another drag on her cig and—a thousand blessings on her tobacco-addicted head—pulls out a vaccination card that clearly, definitively, officially indicates that Fido or Fluffy or Vicious Demon Puppy is up to date with all of his shots, rabies included.

Phew!! I'm feeling reassured. The kids are not. They worry that I'll be among the 100 percent of those exposed to rabies who do nothing about it and thus die a slow, horrible death. I tell them no, that won't happen, the dog was vaccinated. For the next day or two, I repeat this mantra over and over and over again: THE DOG WAS VACCINATED. THE DOG WAS VACCINATED. Say it with me! THE DOG WAS VACCINATED.

I'm actually pretty darn lucky, I tell them: After all the strays we've seen in Ecuador, I somehow manage to get bitten by a vaccinated pet. Think about it! It's like winning the lottery! I'm also lucky I'm wearing crop pants that go down to my calf; I'm lucky I lost that really nice pair of shorts I bought several days ago in Portoviejo, because I certainly would have worn them on our last day in Puyo, and I certainly would have wound up with a much more serious injury.

As I say this, I reflect on the crop pants I'm wearing. Ah, yes, I wore them to the monkey refuge earlier in the day. Ah, yes, I'll bet I stink of those thieving little buggers: No wonder the German Shepherd attacked me. Here I mention, not quite in passing, that this is the second time in three months I've been bitten by a dog. The last one ran right up to me on the sidewalk and snapped me in the keister; later, I heard from a knowledgeable source that the dog had been "exhibiting herding instincts recently." So when I don't smell like monkey, I smell like. . . cow? That, or I possess some irresistible animal attraction, although it seems to work exclusively on small, disturbed primates and mentally disordered household pets.

On the long drive back—through the night, over the Andes, penetrating a dense fog that puts visibility at about two feet—Washington, our driver, asks about Chris. Between his broken English and my broken Spanish, we haltingly discuss the vanished man in my life, his illness, his death, my experiences with the children since. I am not sure what prompts Washington to ask, what sets him apart from his countrymen, until he begins to speak of his divorce and his own children. There's a new woman in his life, he says, but nothing matters more to him than the kids.

The conversation doesn't last long, maybe five or ten minutes. But it touches me deeply. My three beauties, asleep in the back, are my entirety. They fill this new world of mine. Their intrepid course through life will carry them past mountain and river and sea, on horses and rafts, through sunshine and clouds. Sometimes I'll be with them. Sometimes I won't. Either way, they own my heart.

And we're a family, still.

31 I Really Need To Say This Out Loud

I won't kill myself. I won't.

I say this aloud, and I have to, because my kids have to hear it. *I* have to hear it. I think back often to my friend Joe, leaning across the loveseat toward me that bright, bleak September afternoon. He was right when he said that no one in a ten-mile radius is less at risk of suicide. He's right because he has to be right, because it has to be true. I know that I can't kill myself, so I won't. So I say that I won't. So I repeat it, loudly, whenever I have to, whenever I sense the kids could use a reminder.

Suicide is a fucker. It just is. After my sister Lucy committed suicide—OD'd on psych meds—I was stunned to realize that some people consider the act a choice, an actual, rational choice, and one of these same people expressed as much to me in soothing tones soon after her death. I couldn't believe what I was hearing. Lucy? The brilliant, Harvard-educated, empathic, loving, giving Lucy? She "chose" to do herself in? To rip our mother's heart out? My heart, too? No. Lucy didn't embrace her suicidality; she didn't *choose* it; she felt it and fought it bravely. Then it vanquished her.

She was out of her head with despair, just as my father, Louis, was out of his head when he made his attempt—OD'd on sleeping pills—and just as my husband was out of his head when he jumped. I sometimes try to put myself in that vacated headspace, wondering why anyone with anything to live for would throw it all away. Chris adored his children as much or more than any man I knew. He was a devoted husband, a generous friend, a man always attentive and attuned to other people's needs. How could he have done this? What could have seized him in that moment? What if he had stepped back from the rim of the parking garage? Would that moment have passed?

This is what suicide does to the ones left behind. The damnation of it, the nasty and never-ending slog if it, is just this sort of fruitless and relentless cross-examination, the serial questioning that never ever yields an answer. Like the guilt, it gets you nowhere. It loops around and around and around, teasing and torturing with the cruelest of all cruel falsehoods: that your loved one might have lived had you only done something differently, or said something differently, or not said something else.

The if-onlys will eat you alive, if you let them. They'll consume you from within. The best you can do, the best *I* can manage, is to lift the rational above the irrational and see this awful questioning as a function of the grief, and then see the grief as a thing apart from myself—my Self. It's noisy, obnoxious, persistent. But it isn't me.

This is me: The one still here. The one who won't kill herself because she knows what it means to lose a dear one to suicide, she knows how it hurts, not for a year or two, but forever. Forever. I won't do that to my own dear ones. I'm not built that way. I bend but don't break; or perhaps I'm already broken, and that's my secret weapon. I learned at age 11, just as my children learned, that a parent can love you but still yield to melancholy. Mine returned to me. Theirs didn't. I don't know why and I never will, no matter how often I ask.

It's not fair. None of it's fair. Every death feels like an injustice to the grieving, but suicide brings on its own sense of wrongness: seven months later, it still throbs and festers with doubt, demanding answers I don't have. There is no figuring this out. I had no chance to say goodbye to Chris at the end, no time for closure, no occasion to say, "I love you, and thank you for all that you gave me." I don't know what he felt as he hurled off his parapet into the blue. I don't know what he saw as he looked down and out and over our bustling, friendly neighborhood that last moment. I don't know whether peace overcame him, or fear, or love. I picture him climbing the stairs to the roof of the parking garage, looking around, choosing a spot. I wonder if he hesitated: did he think of us? I wonder if he looked over the edge and felt seized by dizziness: did he plunge head first? He must have. "Multiple traumatic blunt force injuries," in the words of the death certificate, suggest a vicious descent.

No one will ever ask such questions of me. My loved ones will never have to parse a coroner's phrasings, question my final paroxysms, wonder about my mental state or picture me on a ledge.

I'm not leaving that way. I'm not killing myself. Neither should you.

32 The Hitchhiker

I am now, officially, sick of the grief. Sick of the wailing and griping and grousing. Sick of the Me Me Boring Old Me rattling around aimlessly in the cavernous reaches of my head. I decide, after a couple of whiny phone conversations with a couple of saintly friends, that I want to be a better, less selfish, less complaining, nicer, happier, more helpful and outward-oriented person. I pray for discernment.

This is what Catholics do when they're clueless. They "discern," which means they pray for guidance and insight in whatever form the Holy Spirit might choose to deliver it, be it a conversation with an insightful friend, a "still, small voice" in one's own mind, a remark made in a priest's Sunday homily, or some coded message in an episode of *Modern Family*. It's a form of Roman Catholic F.S.O., this opening-up to outside influences, and lately, addled by my failures to figure my own self out, I've been doing more and more of it. I do my best to listen, and this time, the voice that speaks is a book of short works by Leo Tolstoy that's been gathering dust on my bedroom shelf for who knows how long and somehow, miraculously, catches my eye.

Immediately, I flip it open to the contents page. Immediately, my glance falls on a three-page fable, *The Three Questions*. Immediately, I open it. Read it. Ingest the details of its small, sharp plot, which concerns a king's search for meaning and his time spent digging a hole with a wise man. Basically, the king wants to know the right time to do something, the best people to be with, and the most important thing to do. By digging the hole, which helps the wise man and serendipitously prevents the king from being assassinated, the king learns firsthand the answers to his questions.

The right time to do something is Now, because it's the only time you have any power. The best person to be with is whoever you're with at the moment. And the most important thing to do is whatever helps that person.

Hmmm, I think. Discern *that*.

So I'm driving up Madison Avenue in Albany, thinking about the Now, when I spot a miniature old man with his thumb out. He's across the street from the New York State Museum, not a usual hot spot for hitchhiking. He's wearing a short-waisted army jacket and cap, and he looks to be, oh, 80 years old.

Now, normally I don't pick up hitchhikers. Unless they're women. Or ancient. Then I figure, What the hey, they can't do any major damage to me, and I wouldn't want anyone else picking them up, right? So I pick up the mini old man in the army jacket. He climbs in. He's even tinier up close. He has a big paper shopping bag and laughing eyes that he aims at me with a squint.

I pull over. He climbs in.

Where ya goin', I ask.

"Guilderland. Past Guilderland. Way past Guilderland."

He mentions a town, and inwardly I say: Way, way, *way* past Guilderland. That's an hour and twenty minutes west of Albany. In the middle of nowhere, Mr. MicroHitchhiker. Outwardly I say: I've got kids coming home from school in an hour, so I can't take you all the way there.

He suggests a gas station at an intersection I know, maybe a twenty minute drive. Sure thing, I tell him. We swap names. I'm Amy. He's Al.

We make small talk. Al tells me he hitchhikes into Albany often, about once a week. He goes down to the mission. Do I know it? Of course I know it. What does he do down there?

"I collect things. Pick up things. I'm a collector."

This he says with a nice, soft, downstate "R": "I'm a collectah."

Al tells me he collects old movies, old TV shows, old books and old records, old military stuff. All kinds of old crap. Here he pulls out a DVD boxed set of *Hee Haw*, holds it up with pride and joy.

"See?" he says.

Ah.

Then, describing his jaunts on the road, Al launches into a lengthy disquisition on cops. He names names: which cops are "nice," which cops are MEAN. He tells me, "The cops in the city are nicest. Albany, Schenectady—they're nice. Cops in the small towns, they're MEAN." Some cops harass him. Some do not. Some cops, the MEAN ones, tell him to cease and desist as soon as he sticks out his thumb. Some, the MEANest kind of all, arrest him on the spot. Sometimes he gets dragged before judges. He names their names, too. The nice ones. The MEAN ones. Once, in Cooperstown, an extra-MEAN judge tossed him in jail for eight days.

Eight days?! Seriously? For hitchhiking?

"Yeah. Yeah. He was MEAN, oh boy."

You'd think all these cops and judges would have better things to do, I say.

"You'd think."

I say to myself, I am in the Now! I am being totally and unreservedly present to my passenger! This is good! Yes! Then, suddenly, Al changes the subject. Shoots me another squinty look.

"You from Albany?"

Not originally, I say. Born in Queens, grew up in Connecticut. What about you?

"Born in Brooklyn. Moved up here in '57."

Ah.

Brief pause. I'm driving, of course, but from the corner of my eye I can tell he's sorting me out.

"You said you have kids?"

Yep. 18, 16, 11.

"You have a husband?"

Inwardly I say: Dammit all. If I answer this correctly, it will alter the course of the conversation. It will shift the focus from him to me. Which I would rather not do. Because I am sick of Me. But what the heck. I'm in the Now! Maybe this will go somewhere interesting or engaging or even vaguely helpful. So outwardly I say: I did have a husband. I was married for 20 years. He died in September.

"Cancer?"

That soft downstate "R" again. *Can-suh.* Again I debate whether to answer. Again I decide to respond honestly.

No, I say. No, my husband became suddenly mentally ill and wound up killing himself.

Al's reaction is quick and emphatic.

"Nooooo!" he howls. "I hate that! Not the good ones! Now, I don't care when the MEAN bastards (*"bass-tuhds"*) do it. They can all kill themselves, for all I care! But the good ones, noooo!"

This has never occurred to me before, this distinction between the suicides of nice folk on the one hand, A-holes on the other. I had previously assumed that suicide in general was a bummer. Al has given me moral and spiritual food for thought. But he doesn't give me much time to chew on it, because his quicksilver mind is on the move. He shoots me another squinty look.

"You have a boyfriend?"

Ummm...No. I don't have a boyfriend.

"You don't! Well, I'll be your boyfriend! You want to be my girlfriend? I'LL BE YOUR BOYFRIEND!"

He pats my arm. Several times. Then he strokes it, over and over, up and down, as though applying sunblock. This is the arm currently engaged in shifting the gears on the automobile I am driving, and I can't jerk it away. And so he pats and strokes it. "I'll be your boyfriend! OH, BOY!"

He recites his full name, phone number and address for my future reference. I laugh and say, Oh, Al. I laugh again, a somewhat spastic laugh of embarrassment. Hahahahahah. Thanks, but no thanks, I manage to spit out.

But inwardly I say: Holy holy holy SHIT, it's been a long time since a man has reached for me in this way. Any man! Of any age or size! Even a miniature octogenarian hitchhiker with a *Hee-Haw* boxed set! Then I think: What, am I nuts? To which the answer is: Yes! Yes, I am totally, unambiguously, spectacularly nuts, thank you very much. Grief makes you nuts! Loneliness makes you nuts! The two combined make you want to hump every freaking thing that might hold still for the duration! Evil laugh! Bwahahahaha!

This is something no one discusses about widowhood—the bizarre physical intensity of its grief-stricken spousal loneliness. One feels cleaved in two. One feels deprived of a limb, or several limbs, or all of them plus a nostril. One feels phantom pain, except it isn't phantom; it's real, and it hurts, and I mean that physically. The loss of intimacy and desire to be held become so overpowering that some widows have been known to binge on anonymous sex.

Not me. I'm a nice Catholic girl, so I just pick up diminutive collect-ahs on the side of the road. But this is how I want it. I chose this! This is my life in the Now! Watch me discern! I'm not sure what I'm discerning—aside from Al's amorous good cheer—but at least I've figured out the relative niceness of judges and law enforcement in pockets of upstate New York. That's not nothing. And I've figured out something else, too, something that Chris figured out long before I met him: that strangers, wounded souls, old folks, and odd ducks all have their stories to tell, and if we let them, if we listen, we might learn.

Al rubs my arm again, spitting out his contact info a few more times, thoughtfully remembering to include the area code. In an attempt to deflect him, I ask more questions about his weekly trips to Albany. How long does it take him, usually? Between an hour-fifteen and four, depending. Does he know most of the cops by name between here and there? Sure. He also knows the names of people at various missions and pantries. Some of them are MEAN, too. Turns out he also knows the location, accessibility and tastiness of every single church dinner. Al hates casseroles. They stink, he says. We discuss this for a surprisingly long time. The highlight:

"They smell terrible. Oh, boy."

Ah.

Then he starts telling me about Sister So-and-So, an extra-nice nun who picked him up some years back. She hates the Bishop. Al likes the Bishop, remembers him from his time as a street priest in Albany's South End. I like him, too: He's a good priest and a good man. But Sister So-and-So, she couldn't stand him.

Why not, I ask.

"I don't know. But she hated him, oh, boy. She was married, you know. Sister So-and-So. Before she became a nun."

Al aims yet another squint my way. I can feel it. My skin tingles. I can also feel a comment forming on my tongue that I probably shouldn't utter, but I am in the Now, and the Now's temptations prove formidable.

Ya know, Al. Ya know…I was thinking about becoming a nun someday. After my husband died, I say.

It's my turn to dart him a look. Zap. A flick of the eyes between gear shifts.

What do you think, Al? Should I? Become a nun?

At this, Al nearly explodes out of his seat. "No!!! The Lord has enough nuns!" he says. "He needs more GIRLFRIENDS!"

And I smack my forehead against the steering wheel, gripped by laughter. This is Al's second helping of moral and spiritual food for thought, this news of God's involvement in the dating scene. For me, it's a revelation. And now that I've heard it, I know that it's true. The Lord needs more girlfriends!

When I drop him off at the gas station, he asks for a hug. In the process he tries to plant a wet one on me, but I duck out of the kiss and wave goodbye with a laugh. He waves back. I drive home, grateful for the attention from a primate more advanced than the ones who pawed me in Ecuador. I'm also grateful to be jogged outside of myself, if only for twenty minutes. I had started the day Sick of Me. I'd been trying so hard to peer within that I'd all but jammed my head inside my anus. Grief will do that to you; if you're not careful, you'll end up puckered with self-absorption and folded inside out, unable to face the world. For a while today I faced it. And it grinned back.

The next day, I call up Bob and tell him about the hitchhiker. His reaction, again, is: "HAHAHAHAHAHAHAHAHA!!" Again he almost breaks the phone, and again I love him for it.

33 Things I Can't Say To Your Face, Part III

I keep visiting Betty. Once a week, I aim for. Just as I tried to visit your mother once a week in that same nursing home, all those many years ago, pushing our first two nuggets in a stroller. Sometimes you'd meet us there after work on Friday, and we'd sit with your mom and Betty, who started out as your mother's paid companion but ended up her friend. Our friend. Afterward we'd head off to a fish fry and invite Betty to come along, but she always said no, remember that? I always wondered why. Do you think maybe she didn't like fish?

Then your mother died, and the next year Mitchell was born, and right away Betty saw his resemblance to you. She saw how proud you were to hold him. I never told you her reaction: "Chris got his boy." I said, Oh, Betty, you know he would've been thrilled with another little girl. And she replied, with a wink and a wave of a hand: "Yeah, yeah. But he got his boy."

After Betty's health declined and memory faded, she moved into the nursing home herself—and you brought us all to visit her on Sunday afternoons. These visits were always your idea, because you were the one, not me, to remember those in need. It was you who arranged our stints at the soup kitchen. You who invited the lonely, the struggling, the hard-up to dinner in our home. It was you who taught us all to look outward, to think beyond the bubble of our own friends and family and see how we might help. I never thanked you for that. I never thanked you for loving not just me and our children, but everyone else, too—everyone at the periphery who needed a lift or a buck. You gave me so much, my darling. You showed me how to love others in your absence, and what more lasting gift could you have left me?

And so I visit Betty when I can. Today, as usual, she asks about you.

"How is Chris?" she asks. "Did he find a job?"

Yes, I say. He found a job.

"And is he happy?"

Yes, I say. He's happy.

She pauses.

"So he's happy at his job?"

I pause.

Yes. He's happy at his job.

"Good."

We both pause.

"Men are strange," she says.

I don't know where this comes from, but I agree. They are strange, I say. They don't always know themselves. They don't always know what they're feeling. They seem afraid to know.

She looks at me and says nothing.

We're supposed to be the emotional ones, I add. The women. But at least we make sense of ourselves. At least we're not afraid to understand the things we feel.

She looks at me and says still more of nothing. I take this as assent. Or possibly confusion. But I'm going with assent.

"Chris got a job?"

Yes.

I look at Betty, a woman somewhere in her well-powdered nineties, eyes cloudy but direct, hair done up in curls. This must have been her day at the nursing home salon.

You look good, I say.

"I'm in a sour mood today."

Why?

She says nothing. I ask again: Why are you in a sour mood?

"So Chris is happy?"

Chris is happy, I confirm, though she can tell that I'm not. Her face is worried, wondering, but I won't explain myself today. These visits hurt. And yet, I need them. She needs them. Today she's in her wheelchair in the hallway, in a dark blue polyester blouse and matching pants. Patients sit. Nurses scurry.

"You need a haircut," she tells me. "You should keep it short."

The girls want me to grow it a bit.

"They're wrong."

I laugh. She says this again. "They're wrong. Keep it short."

Whatever you say. You're the boss.

"How's the neighborhood."

Betty always asks this question, never with a question mark. The neighborhood is good, I tell her. New couples moving onto the street. New babies being born. And the kids are all well.

"They're all in school?"

I give her a rundown: Mitchell's in 6th grade, Jeanne in 10th. I tell her we all visited Madeleine in Ecuador, and she'll be coming home soon. The information blows past Betty without being absorbed, and so I say it again.

Madeleine graduated high school and went to Ecuador. Can you believe it? Ecuador. Next she'll be at Georgetown.

She pauses. She still hasn't absorbed it. Then: "Your hands are cold," she says.

They're always cold.

"Mine are warm."

Yes, they are. Always.

We hold hands. The heat from her skin warms mine.

You're so pretty, I say.

"*You're* so pretty. Does Chris tell you that?"

Yes, I assure her.

(And yes, you used to. But of course you haven't told me in a very long time.)

She smiles.

Betty, I say. You are beautiful. You light up my day. I love visiting you.

"You're my angel."

You're my angel.

"Chris has a job? And he's happy?"

Chris has a job. And he's happy.

She looks at me critically.

"You need a haircut."

Afterward, I walk through the parking lot and feel lighter than I have in weeks. I don't know why. I hate nursing homes. They stink of shit, disinfectant, and overcooked food. But I love Betty. I love that she's known us so long, remembers our early married years so well, remembers our kids as bright-cheeked little ones in training pants. She knows how happy we once were. She remembers all your quirks and imperfections and bouts of willfulness, and she remembers the effects they had on me. She remembers mine and the effects they had on you. She remembers your handsomeness, your strength, the way you once looked at me with amazement and desire. She remembers how I once looked at you with the same.

At my car, I pull out my keys, then stop. I don't know why, but I keep on walking. I walk through this parking lot and then part of a second and then a third. I walk toward the parking garage at the far side. I think to myself, God only knows why I'm doing this, and I mean this literally. God only knows a lot of things. Most things. A few insignificant things I claim to know, but 99 percent of it: God.

I pass a security guy in a car. He gives me a wary look, and I shuffle past. What does he think I'm doing here? Something criminal? I realize I must look guilty. I try to walk less self-consciously. I amble. Ramble. Mosey. One foot, and then the other, and then the other, and then I'm at the base of the parking garage, and I plop myself down on the thick beam of a wooden fence, next to a car.

I study this ugly thing, this bland utilitarian product of our automotive culture, a nondescript stack of poured concrete — three thick layers of it. It's too much to call it a building, but it stakes a greedy claim on its environment. It takes up too much space. I stare up at it. It's too squat to loom, but the blue sky hangs above it with unexpected nearness. Birds sing. A breeze shushes hair into my eyes. A car goes past, and I gaze at my feet. What would the driver think of this tired-looking forty-eight-year-old woman, staring up at the roof of a parking garage?

If only I smoked. Smoking gives loiterers a reason to stand outside and stare at nothing. If only this thing I stare at, now, were truly nothing.

After a few minutes, I get up off the beam and walk toward the garage entrance, still not knowing why. You can't imagine, can you, how the whys pile on and on, each one weighing more than I can carry. So I don't. I shove them off. I cannot deal with whys, and I reject them. This one included. I don't know what force or impulse prods me up three flights to the roof of the parking garage. The first few steps, I think of you. Then my thoughts wander, as they do on any windy day in early spring, and my mind is filled with a catchy, anthemic pop tune I just heard, something about youth and drunkenness and setting the world on fire. I shove that aside, too. I think of you again and take more steps. Feet scrape on cement until I reach the top and, still feeling inexplicably light, I walk out onto the southeast corner of the roof.

It's all but empty. Only a few cars are parked there, at the far northern end. I look to the west and see the Helderberg Escarpment, its ridge a shelf on the horizon, where we often hiked the Indian Ladder Trail. To the south I see the Catskills. I take a deep breath and marvel at the clarity of the day and the beauty of the cosmos and I say, aloud: Isn't this gorgeous. Isn't this gorgeous.

I consider the southern wall of the roof, the side that abuts the parking lot. Then I stop and think: No. Rows of cars are directly below. That would be a problem, wouldn't it, sweetheart? My gaze turns to the eastern wall of the garage. Nothing on that side but an empty access road. For a moment, just a moment, barely even a moment, I stand on my toes out of curiosity—what did you see? how did you see it?—and peer over the edge. I back down and away, rattled. It's higher up here than I thought. From below a three-story garage isn't much, vertiginously speaking. From up top it's something. I don't know what. But something.

I think of you again. When I think of you, nowadays, I'm not sure what I'm thinking, or how. Mostly I see you, all of you, from your blunt powerful form in a polo shirt to your bemused smile and ambiguously colored eyes. Sometimes I can't see you at all, but I remember how it felt to touch you. Sometimes I just see parts. I remember your large and thickly muscled hands. Your tall, broad forehead. Your perfectly formed rosebud mouth. The wrinkles around your ears, the thickness around your middle: I remember that, too. I remember not everything but enough to keep your essence within reach. I wonder how you think of me these days.

Standing on the roof, I say the Our Father and head down the stairwell to the parking lot. This is my exit, not yours. Mine is prosaic and slow. Yours was ghastly and quick.

I haven't learned anything new today. No, I haven't figured you out; I don't know which thoughts coursed through your embattled mind in your last breath, and I never will. But having stared straight down the drop that killed you, I'm even more sure of my own thoughts and my own breath. No. I won't do that. No ledge of any kind will tempt me. Ever.

34 Alone with Electra

One evening, Jane shows up at my door in a little black dress and heels. She often shows up at my door, though she isn't normally dressed to the nines. Tonight is different. Tonight the kids are all up at sleep-away camp on Lake George. Madeleine, home from Ecuador, is a counselor there for the summer. Jeanne is a counselor in training for three weeks. Mitchell is a camper for two.

I've been all alone. Alone! In a way I haven't been since 1988—the last time I lived by myself for any length of time. The house is empty when I leave. It's empty when I return. Even when I'm there, it's empty, because occupancy requires more than one soul at a time to enliven a space and give it character and shape. Without my husband, the house was emptier than it had ever been, but without any of my children, it is a void. And into this void I fall, fall, hitting no bottom because no bottom exists, no bottom could exist, no bottom should. I knock around the walls on my descent.

I slam into the guilt again and again, hard. I slam into the loneliness, just as hard. At each collision I weep into a puddle of tears and snot, and I say, aloud, I DON'T NEED THIS SHIT! because I know I don't. I am self-aware enough to know my guilt is irrational, to know I didn't actually kill my husband. But the shit lands when and where it lands. The grief does what it does. And I lean into it, praying for the peace of God which transcends all understanding while I slog through this steaming pile of crap that I call pain.

This being alone. I don't like it, I haven't figured it out, and I don't want to. Before I fell in love with Chris, I knew how to be alone; I was good at it. I had my work, my family and friends, books to read, movies to see, music to play. Life was full without him. But then it wasn't, because he expanded and filled it, and then he expanded and filled it more, always more. Then he left, and only my children can keep this rich world he gave me from feeling vacant.

I still have my work, my family and friends, books to read, movies to see, music to play. But with the kids gone, it's not enough. *I'm* not enough.

I call and email friends, make arrangements for lunch or dinner or some cultural outing. Hey, why not! I say. The kids aren't here! Watch me live it up, amigos! I go to a play with my friend Kathy—a musical channeling Ella Fitzgerald that jolts me awake with electric, kick-ass vigor. The next night I go to a dance recital with Jane—Bill T. Jones at Jacob's Pillow.

So there's Jane, in her little black dress and heels. I am not wearing a little black dress and heels. I am wearing a blouse and capris. She looks at me, says, "Am I overdressed?" and when I murmur something noncommittal, she adds, "You should change."

What do you mean I should change?

"You should put on a dress."

What do you mean I should put on a dress?

"Because if you don't, we'll look like a lesbian couple," she says, and I look down at myself. She is absolutely correct. In this moldy stereotype, she'd be the girly half. Yep. And so I change.

I assume, when I am out with Jane, whether alone or with our kids, whether buying a Christmas tree or inhaling German food at a downtown Bierhaus, that we are mistaken for a couple. I wouldn't normally give a shit, but as Jane puts it, "This is not the look we're going for right now." I do not have a shred of lesbianism in me and sometimes wish I did. It would be easier. I could follow up on that cute little waitress who gave me the once-over at a bistro last week. "We could both do worse," Jane says, and we laugh. She, too, is rather adamantly straight.

As for me, I could not be straighter. I have had crushes on males since age 3, and I am not exaggerating. The first was Alex, a boy I worshipped in nursery school. He ignored me. So I smeared paint all over his paintbox, and then he hated me. Then came Mike. He ignored me. So I punched him in the stomach on the playground, and then he hated me. Then came Brian. He ignored me. I would like to say I made him hate me at some point, but I cannot, because I failed to register with him on any plane. That's OK, because he had muscles, and I soothed myself by staring at them a lot. Several chaps I admired in the years that followed also had muscles, from Tarzan, to the Six Million Dollar Man, to Captain Kirk, to my treasured husband — his build acquired through weightlifting, and before that, years of carpentry.

At some point in my lifelong appreciation of beefcake I realized I had a pretty bad case of the Electra complex. I considered, in a rare moment of honest Freudian reflection, that my father was a muscular writer with bad handwriting. My husband was a muscular writer with bad handwriting. All my life, I have been attracted to muscular writers with bad handwriting.

I confess this to my shrink. She muses, "Well, this will simplify things. Whenever you're ready to date, just run a personal ad saying, `WIDOW WITH THREE KIDS SEEKS MUSCULAR WRITER WITH BAD HANDWRITING.' "

Great idea.

At Jacob's Pillow, jointly overdressed with my non-lesbian friend, Jane, I do not find any muscular writers with bad handwriting. Instead I find many old Berkshires residents in pale-blue polo shirts and sleeker New Yorkers in blacker clothes.

But I am not here to man-scope. I am here to see Bill T. Jones, the great dancer/choreographer. Before the concert, I explain to Jane that I haven't seen Jones since the late 70s, when he spent one fall as an artist-in-residence at the small girls' school in Connecticut where my mother taught music and I met the Richardsons. Jane spots him on the festival grounds. We ooze over.

Mr. Jones, I say, sticking out my hand and introducing myself. Mr. Jones, I was a student at Wykeham Rise.

He smiles — a big one, genuine. He remembers the place.

I want to thank you, I say. Because you came to my soccer practice at Wykeham. You told me I moved well. When you said that, it changed me forever, gave me confidence, shaped my life.

He smiles again — another big one.

"I'm glad," he says. "When you say something to someone, and it happens to be the right moment..."

It *was* the right moment. It shaped me, I say again. I became confident. I played soccer all through college.

A third big smile.

"No injuries?" he asks.

Ahhh, my knees are shot, I say. I laugh at this. He laughs, too. He has a gorgeous laugh, full-throated and warm.

I thank him again and say goodbye. Jane and I ooze away.

I say to myself: Holy shit! I just thanked Bill T. Jones in person! I've ALWAYS wanted to thank Bill T. Jones in person!...*I can't wait to call Chris and tell him*!

Then this irrational thought, traveling a habitual neural pathway, screeches to halt. And I think: Dammit dammit dammit. There is no Chris to call.

Later, Jane and I watch Jones's troupe perform. The magnificent, willowy choreographer reads from a selection of his life's stories while knotty young dancers writhe and clench around him.

It is strange and mesmerizing, full of memory and mystery and loss. My breath catches. My eyes water. I wonder at art, at its ability to touch us and our willingness to be touched; if we refuse to let it in, its beauty does nothing, means nothing, fails to move. To live and love, we must lower our defenses. We must receive. We must say, All right, life, all right, art, all right, fellow piddling humans, go ahead do your best or worst to me. Make me feel something, anything, a thing that feeds or changes me or brings me closer to some truth.

I don't know what that truth is. Maybe it's simply the promise of all great art; that none of us is alone, even when we suffer. Especially when we suffer. Perhaps that's when we're *least* alone—in the dark, mulling all we've lost—because that's when we're most truly human. It's like that old song by the Police, "Message in a Bottle": our loneliness unites us on our separate beaches, in a minor key, with a driving backbeat. But most of the time we don't hear it. Deaf to the paradox, we need art to remind us that we're not alone in being alone.

35 New Amy Loads the Dishwasher

Amy without Chris is different from Amy with Chris. Socially, she is a whole new creature. She utters every damn thought that crosses her mind, so long as it's true. She swears a shitload more than she used to: bad words shoot from her mouth unbidden, like the noxious and fiery ejecta from some long-dormant, unusually short volcano, or the pus from an unusually tall zit. ("Mom," observes Mitchell, "You say the S-word a *lot*.")

New Amy worries less, or not at all, about what people think of her. She second-guesses herself less. She interrupts more. She feels much more at ease in her own skin, much more fearless, much more confident—or no, it's not that she's confident. She still has a chronically low opinion of herself. It's that she just doesn't *care*. When you're in this kind of pain, and for so long, nothing else can hurt you, really. As she explains to the children, "Only the end of the world is the end of the world. And even that's the start of something new."

Amy without Chris still misses her husband terribly. She wishes with every wriggling cell in her body that she were still Amy with Chris. But she's not. She can't move forward without acknowledging that she's not. No matter how often her friends say, Amy, You Won't Be Alone Forever, or Amy, You'll Find Another Good Mr. Manly Pants, the fact of the matter is that right now, there is no Mr. Manly Pants. Right now, she's just her own little self. And her own little self has, in recent months, become much, much more blunt. *"Bluntissimo,"* coins my friend, Bev, a choral director.

I have always apologized a lot. A ridiculous lot. Lately I have decided to ditch this habit, because A) it's pointless; B) it tends to bug the people I love; C) I often find myself apologizing for apologizing, a stupidly meta exercise in guilt inflation that can go on forever; and D) it's pointless.

A scant week after Chris died, my dad left a couple of messages before I was able to call him back. When we finally spoke, he cut me off before I could spit out some idiotic mea culpa for being hard to reach.

"Amy," he said. "Are you about to apologize? Because if you apologize, I'm going to come out there and shit on your head."

A hollow threat. But still.

So the New Amy plans to disgorge fewer sorries than the Old Amy, or so I declare to myself and everyone who'll listen.

A fine occasion for me to test this resolve is my parents' 50th anniversary party.

They've booked a leafy old inn in Vermont for the weekend, and most everyone will be there: Dan (Dad), Pat (Mom), their daughter, Betsy, their sons, Danny and Randy, their families, and a few close friends. Plus their non-blood progeny: Connie and her daughter, and me, and Nils. Nils is approximately the nicest person on the planet and someone who apologizes as much as I do, maybe more. I look forward to trying out my new sorry-less persona in his presence.

I agree to arrive at the hotel by 3 on Friday. I pull up at 3:08. There's my dad in his massive Honda Pilot, Nils beside him. Dad rolls down the window, wags me over with his finger. I get out.

"You're late," he says.

I know, I say.

"Aren't you going to apologize?"

No, I say.

"Don't you feel guilty?"

No, I say.

He gives me an incredulous but happy look. Nils is laughing.

"So you're *not* going to say you're sorry?"

Nope. This is the New Me, I explain—and the New Me doesn't apologize. So watch out, I tell him.

And the incredulous, happy look becomes an enormous smile.

All day he tests me, trying to get me to apologize. He gets nowhere.

New Amy refuses to take the blame for anything. New Amy is resolute. New Amy is bold. New Amy cracks inappropriate jokes. New Amy is also hunk-o-man-hungry; she jokes to her parents that she plans to pick up a "random" at some wedding party being held at the inn, even though she doesn't believe it herself. They clearly don't believe her, either (HA HA HA HA that's funny, Amy, HA HA HA go pick up a guy HA HA HA HA HA), and for good reason, as Old Amy continues to take the upper hand when it comes to sexual morality. New Amy does not even attempt to swipe some New Mr. Manly Pants from his plate of beef tenderloin medallions under the tent.

But the sorries! I will have you know that New Amy does an excellent job quashing the sorries. All day, my dad tries to prod a reflexive apology out of me, and all day, I resist. He asks if he should wear long pants or shorts, and I say shorts, but then I selfishly change into capris before dinner. He gives me shit for this.

"Don't you feel guilty for making me wear shorts, and then changing out of them yourself?"

No, I say.

"You won't say sorry?"

No, I say.

Go, New Amy! Go, New Amy!

This continues through Friday evening and Saturday morning. It goes on until, obeying some rare and uncharacteristic domestic-

cleaning impulse, I take it upon myself to load the dishwasher in
my parents' hotel condo. Unfortunately, I space out and
accidentally load it with concenfuckingtrated Tide, then turn it
on and leave for a hike with the clan. Have you ever loaded a
dishwasher with concenfuckingtrated Tide, either accidentally or
on purpose? No? Well, this is what happens. THE
DISHWASHER VOMITS SOAP.

On our return from the hike, Nils stumbles across this
interesting scientific fact. He walks into the kitchenette, screams
HOLY SHIT!! and then returns from the kitchenette with his feet
encased in concenfuckingtrated-soap-lather so colossal that he
seems to be wearing fluffy white moon boots. The suds reach
halfway to his knee. At this point, the only thing for me to do is
to yell OH MY GOD!! while falling to the floor with towels
alongside Nils, who laughs and tells me he did something
similar to a similar Richardson dishwasher a few decades earlier.

All I can say is, HA HA YOU'RE KIDDING and THANK
YOU FOR HELPING, NILS, and HOLY SHIT!! and then of
course I AM SO SORRY I AM SO SO SO SORRY SORRY SORRY
SORRY SORRY SORRY, this last string of apologies directed at
my parents. Who are laughing. At me. And at the complete
collapse of my newfound resolve to Not Express Remorse.

But flooding the kitchen surely merits an apology, I say. On
this point, Dad yields. Later, after the rest of the family has
arrived for the party, Danny tells me I shouldn't apologize at all.
For the dishwasher, or anything else. Ever again.

"You know what you have to say when Dad gives you
shit." This is more of a declaration than a question. I prep to
receive this incoming dose of brotherly wisdom.

What's that, I reply.

"Bite me."

I've never been clear on the origin and meaning of this
phrase (bite which part of me, exactly, and for that matter do I
really want to be bitten?), but I try it out and repeat it at Danny's
instruction. I like how it feels. I like the percussive smack on my

lips. I especially like the madcap invitation to *outré* dental violence. Old Amy never told anyone to bite her! No way! Then again, Old Amy was never attacked in the thigh by a deranged Ecuadorian German Shepherd.

It occurs to me that New Amy is markedly more Richardsonian than Old Amy ever was; that would certainly explain the uptick in profanity. I had always felt at home with these folks. I had always walked into Dan and Pat's house without knocking—and what better, clearer affirmation of family love and acceptance can we ask for? In figuring out the shit of my new self, I figured out this: not merely that I love them, which I knew, and I need them, which I recognize, but I'm one of them. Which is obvious.

New Amy says: OK, so what the hell. Bite me.

36 W.G.W.

On Saturday night, before the anniversary dinner, I have a fascinating conversation with my old friend, Hayden. I've known Hayden since he was a squirt. Now a tall man with a brisk intelligence and wry wit, he says anything and everything on any possible subject that bubbles up. We discuss my recent personality change. It turns out he is pleased to accommodate New Amy on her quest to be obnoxious.

"You know what you have to do tonight," he says. Again the declarative tone. Again I prepare to receive a dollop of masculine wisdom.

What's that, I say.

"You have to get drunk."

Oh, I do! I respond, my eyes widening. Absolutely, Hayden! I *have to get drunk*! Of course!! It's a plan!!!

Why has this not occurred to me before? What an ingenious new spin on F.S.O.! Old Amy *never* got drunk! This is surely one area where New Amy can expand her horizons, especially with the kids off at sleepaway camp. The weekend bash in Vermont provides a most excellent opportunity for me to explore and experiment in new and exciting ways. I just have to figure out how. When I say Old Amy never got drunk, I mean Old Amy never got drunk. OK, so maybe I got a little happy on Kahlúa with Pam that one time in the winter of 1988, but not enough to cause a hangover. So at the pre-dinner gathering with hors d'oeuvres, I have a little wine. Over dinner, I have a little more wine. At the post-dinner gathering in Randy's room, I have a glass of beer.

I am so, so proud of myself. I'm drinking! I think. I'm actually drinking! Go, New Amy! Go, New Amy!

Of course, all of this drinking—"all" of this "drinking"—has occurred over a five-hour span, so I am not technically drunk. I am not even technically buzzed. Just lubricated a bit around the joints and eyeballs. But it's nice.

At Randy's we play Uno. If you know that card game, you know that it is very, very simple. It is a game seemingly designed for preschoolers and inebriates, and it is based on chance. The goal is to run out of cards. The cards themselves are also very, very simple, consisting primarily of numbers in blue, yellow, green and red. Additional cards can skip players, reverse directions or require the player sitting next to you to pick up yet more cards: +2, +4. One can only use the hated +4 card on one's neighbor in direst circumstances, that is, when one has no other option, and one must do so with full understanding that the preschooler or inebriate you've just nailed with the +4 will exact revenge in the future.

It is a beastly thing to do to a fellow human being, the +4. Remember this later.

Randy and his wife, Susi, welcome the post-bash crowd into their digs at the inn. We join them in a circle around the coffee table: To my right sits Danny's son, Walker. To my left, Nils. Remember this later, too. And remember what I said about Nils being approximately the nicest person on the planet.

As Randy doles out the cards, the morbid quippery begins immediately.

Back home, few people make light of my loss. I worry, each time I nose my way through a crowd, that the crowd looks back and sees my husband standing at my shoulder. Or some other body part: maybe they picture him riding piggyback, looping an arm around my neck or gnawing at my ear. Perhaps he's merely a shimmer, an afterimage that gleams and sticks to the eyelids. But he's there. As hard as I've worked at figuring and formulating a New Amy who can stand on her own without him, I suspect that Chris will always be present to others; his death left me alone while planting him firmly beside me. I'm widowed too precipitously, and too soon, for anyone's comfort. Who would dare give me shit about it?

I'll tell you who. The Richardsons.

Here in this little Vermont inn, the indecorous widow jokes are flying fast and furious, and I realize—with a semi-demi-nowhere-near-drunken surge of gratitude—that my current grieving status is only a temporary thing to this group of loving, straight-talking, generous-hearted people, most of whom have known me for thirty-five years. They knew me as a kid with bangs and braces. They knew me long before I met Chris, got married, lost my parents and sister, had kids. Then lost Chris, too.

They knew me before all of that. To them I'm just Ames. To them, I've always been just Ames, neither less nor more, and I always will be. So no one looks at me over their beer and Uno cards and sees the ghost of my dead husband. They look over and see an old friend doing her best to live and love and lumber through her latest personal mountain of shit. And so they help me through it.

Sometime during the first hand, Hayden regards me calmly and makes an especially apt and cutting remark. I don't remember how it starts, but I remember how it finishes: "Widow gets wasted," he declares.

I love it! Widow gets wasted! W.G.W! Yes! Go, New Amy!

It sounds like an old Pearl Jam song, I say. I start singing a slow, grinding ballad in a minor key with accompanying air guitar: "Widow...widow gets *waaaayyysssted.*"

Randy whips out his iPhone and Googles it. "Let's see if there's actually a song called 'Widow Gets Wasted,'" he says, and I am confident the Interwebs have never before been used for such a noble task. A few seconds later, he reports back: In fact, there's a rock band named Wasted Widow.

I think, Of course there is!! There had to be!! Then I think, What the hell??

It has a website, www.wastedwidow.com, which, as I later learn in my search for information, offers nothing but the band's name in bloody typeface over what appears to be a snake-eyed zombie's head. Their MySpace page is a bit more extensive and offers a sampling of tunes, including a little number called "Adios Bitches" that sounds like heavy machinery dragging construction workers to their deaths in a gravel pit also occupied by incubi and succubi hooked up to guitar-feedback loops. After three minutes of this, your brain will start seeping out your ears. I'm not kidding.

But back to the Uno game, where "wasted widow" jokes are now bouncing around the circle like silicone implants at Cocoa Beach. New Amy laughs at all of them. New Amy quaffs her beer and throws down her Uno cards, a red "7" here, a blue "skip" there, and the night progresses happily from one hand to another.

Then, at around 11 p.m., she gets dealt a hand with a +4 card. Very soon she is forced to use it. On Nils. Who is, as I'll say for the third time here, approximately the nicest person on the planet. Who would not hurt a soul. Even if it were a really, really mean soul who hurt him first and maybe even unexpectedly stabbed him in the arm with a fork. New Amy deeply regrets this +4 card she inflicts on him, but she has no choice.

Sorry Nils, I say.

Nils laughs. He always laughs, even with a fork dangling from his tricep. Randy says something about the Wasted Widow sticking it to Nils. And then we all laugh! Ha ha ha ha!

The hand progresses. I quaff more beer. I get another +4 which, again, I am forced to use. On Nils.

Go, New Amy! Go, Wasted Widow! Ha ha ha!

The hand progresses further. I quaff yet more beer. I get yet another +4, which, once again, I am forced to use. On Nils.

NILS NILS NILS I AM SOOOOO SORRY, says the Wasted Widow, and at this point he really would be better off if I just stabbed him in the arm with flatware. After getting hit with three +4s in a row, Nils now has so many cards he could leave and start his own game somewhere else, like maybe that wedding party from which I failed to score a Manly Pants the night before.

Randy leans toward Nils, waggles his eyebrows. He is a master eyebrow waggler. "The wasted widow?" he asks, cocking his head. "Or is she just...?" He grunts briefly. Nils laughs. I laugh, too. I am not sure what the grunt signifies, but it's not nice.

A few minutes later, it's my turn again. I have no cards to put down, not a one. And so I am forced to draw. I get a +4. As the game progresses around the circle, I pray that someone will reverse direction, *please please please please*. No one does.

My turn again. I have no options left. According the rules of the game, I am once more compelled to screw over Nils with a +4. Or am I?

Hmmmm, maybe I'll just pretend I don't have it. Why not? No one would be the wiser, right? Unless of course Walker, off to my right, happens to glimpse my hand and see the evil +4 lurking within.

"Hey!" he yells. "Hey! You have a +4! Amy has a +4!"

No, I don't! No, I don't! New Amy is sick and tired of sticking it to Nils! This isn't a +4 in my hand, it's...it's...an astral projection of all the other +4s that I previously used in sticking it to Nils!

"You have it! You HAVE TO USE IT!" Walker insists.

And so I am forced to use a +4. On Nils. For the fourth time. Who is, for the fourth time, approximately the nicest person on the planet.

Again Randy leans toward Nils, quirking the eyebrows. He is a master eyebrow quirker. "Nils," he says. "Nils. She is such a *bitch!*"

The circle erupts with raucous laughter, none louder than mine. This is a wondrous and epochal milestone in my grief. In the last ten months, no one has thought to address me this way.

I thank Randy from the bottom of my heart. See, everyone at home tells me how much they admire me, I explain. People come up to me with wet eyes and awe. Being called "bitch"? *This* is a *vast* improvement.

He throws me a huge smile. They all do. Widow gets wasted! Widow gets wasted!

Well, not so much. But the bitch is pooped, so she says good night. "The Wasted Widow is weaving," Danny declares. And thus she makes her departure, the New Amy hoarse from laughing.

 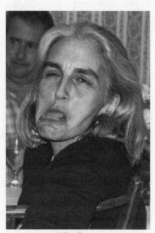

Before the widow gets wasted...   **and after...**

37 Memo to Clooney Redux

To: George Clooney
From: No One You Know
Re: *The Descendants*

Everyone says you look like me. No, wait: They say *I* look like *you*. Or they say you look like my brother, but they never say which brother of mine you look like, and frankly, you don't look like any of them, especially the one with the muscles and hoop earrings who resembles Mr. Clean. It's possible I look like your sister, but I haven't seen her: Is there a similarity? I'd run a search on Google Images, but I don't want her to feel stalked. Friends who've seen pictures of my late father tell me you two resemble each other, and aside from your sorry lack of a most prominent and excellent Roman nose, I would agree.

My friend Jane accuses me of being in love with you, and that is SO NOT TRUE. For the record, I don't find you attractive at all! In any reproductive or libidinal sense! No offense! Not in *that* way, Mr. Clooney. My Electra complex isn't *that* bad. But I can't persuade her otherwise. She's convinced that my admiration for you and your movies—all of my many positive reviews over the years—mean that, deep down, I nurse some longstanding giggly-girly crushy-wushy thing. And I don't. Honest. I don't.

What I'm feeling, of late, is straight-up amazement. I keep thinking about *The Descendants*, and I need to know: How, sir, did you come to embody the inner life of an exhausted widower with such a potent admix of exasperation and tenderness? When you've barely even been married yourself? Yeah, yeah, yeah, so you're an actor, so I've heard, and that's what actors do, embody feelings outside their own experience, yeah, yeah, yeah, I've heard that, too. But I don't buy it. What you did in that movie was something above and beyond the usual actor's craft. You didn't just ape the emotions of a person wracked with heartache, confusion, fatigue. You became that person. You became me.

That scene at your comatose wife's bedside? When you said, with such perfect, pained surrender, "Goodbye, my friend, my joy, my pain, goodbye, goodbye, goodbye"? That's what I said in silence at my husband's open casket before the wake. That's what I said as he lay there, his cold, beautiful, broken face soon to be hidden from mourners. That's what I said that first night he was dead, and I slept with my children on the living room floor. We couldn't sleep apart that night. After six months of the strangest, blackest nightmare, six months of losing him slowly and watching him drift away, his sudden grisly death pitched us into a state even stranger and blacker—because we knew it was a beginning as well as an end. Because we knew it was real.

That's what you nailed in *The Descendants*, this perplexed arrival at some new and foreign place, with new and foreign rules and responsibilities. When your character admitted to his kids that he didn't know which day the pool guy comes, I roared in sympathy. FIGURE SHIT OUT, George! F.S.O.!

I was watching at home, and thank God for that. I wasn't assigned to it review it, and thank God for that, too. No way I could have coughed up a review with anything approaching objectivity, always a lofty goal for critics paid to pop off. That movie reduced me to a slobbering, blathering, honking, mucus-ejecting mess. How'd you do it? How does any actor do anything that makes a viewer laugh or cry? When you learn your lines and hit your marks just right, you speak and walk for us. This is the true magic of cinema, not all the blinged-out effects: instead it's those pithy, passing moments that resonate in the audience's gut with oomph and authenticity. They won't hit all of us every time. But when they do, and we're sitting on our couches with tears down our cheeks and chills up our spines, then all we can say is: Clooney. Bro. You *fucking* nailed it.

You didn't always. How you used to twitch and bob your head! But you knew that already, because I told you as much back on September 26, 1997—fourteen years to the day before my husband killed himself. The medium for this message was my review of *The Peacemaker*, a boring, drecky action film that had you running around in a tizzy after stolen nukes when you weren't weeble-wobbling your face at Nicole Kidman. I was a fan of *E.R.* at the time, and while I liked your rumbling voice and raffish presence, I wanted to smack you upside the head every time you leaned over and made like some idiot feathered drinking bird. I expressed this frustration to the babysitter (a smart, sassy gal to whom I fed French existentialist masterworks) before leaving for the *Peacemaker* screening that night, and she suggested I count the number of times you nodded.

I did. Final tally: 23.

The ensuing review, which ran in the Albany *Times Union*, is notable for two reasons. One, because I addressed it as an open memo to you, George Clooney, imploring you to stop shaking your damned head. And two, because I misspelled "tics" as "ticks," which made me sound like A) a boob and B) a nurse grappling with a school-wide parasite infestation ("And the ticks, George. Get rid of them"). But I like to think you read it. I like to think you saw through the spelling errors and snotty sarcastic take-downs to my genuine concern. As I said:

> Give the action films a rest for a while, George. Play warmer roles in smaller movies, and trust yourself to fill the screen. You look good; you speak well; work at it, and someday you might become a fine cinematic actor. Just stand still.

You accomplished all of these things. I don't actually believe I'm the cause—and the patronizing tone nauseates me a bit, no, more than a bit, well, quite a lot, really—but the childish part of me still likes to take credit for your career. And why shouldn't I! Someone has to take credit for it! Including the Oscar! That is, someone aside from you.

So there you stand, quietly, tic-lessly, opening your pores and letting the sadness flow both ways. Intake and outtake, absorbed and discharged. I don't know if you're feeling it as it passes through you. I don't know if it's yours—if the origin lies deep within—or if it's borrowed and handled gently from a loved one's store of grief. Your sister is a widow; I know that much about her. Did you observe it in her, feel it with her, skim it off the surface of her pain?

However you came by it, this sadness is genuine, not synthetic. It's generated somewhere, by someone, hurting from something. And with *The Descendants*, I claim it as mine.

Jeanne watched the movie just a few days after I did, and I joined her for the last scene. As the protagonist and his daughters ate ice cream in front of the boob tube—watching *March of the Penguins* from their seats on the couch in the new normal—Jeanne turned to me.

"That's us," she said.

Yep.

"With the ice cream."

Yep.

"After Dad died, watching TV on the couch."

Yep.

"Except with us, it was *Battlestar Galactica*."

Yep.

She turned her gaze back to the screen. If only you had seen her seeing you being us. If only you had seen her bemused expression, filled with the same soft wonder that I felt when I first watched.

"What a great movie," she said.

And I said: Yep.

38 The Checkout Line Jollies, Part II

The more I travel through this zany land of widowhood, the less predictable I become. New Amy sometimes shocks me with her behavior, exhibiting traits that seem to spring from heretofore unseen depths of eccentricity, audacity, and all-around unhinged loose-lippedness. She really does say anything to anyone at any time, and she really doesn't care how anyone reacts.

I don't know what to make of it. It's liberating, I guess. It's also a little freakish. Picture yourself owning a body part that operates without your say-so, like that movie about the pothead kid whose hand just independently goes around killing people. Except in my case, it's my mouth. And as far as I know, it's not killing people.

The story of Amy's Mouth begins with a photo frame. All I need is a photo frame. Not an expensive one, either; a cheap one will do. I simply want to collect some loose family pictures into one modest frame for my bedroom. It's a pleasant enough day, and the dollar store is only a ten-minute walk.

As soon as I enter, I sense something brewing at checkout. The proprietor, a hulking sort with flashing eyes, is staring down a young man at the counter. Walking past them, I hear something about rudeness. Something about money. And then it begins.

"YOU FUCKING PIECE OF SHIT. YOU FUCKING PIECE OF SHIT," shouts the proprietor.

"Fuck you," the young man says with peculiar calm. "Fuck you."

"GET OUT OF MY STORE, YOU FUCKING PIECE OF SHIT, AND NEVER COME BACK."

The young man doesn't move.

"YOU FUCKING PIECE OF SHIT! YOU FUCKING PIECE OF SHIT!"

Nope. Not moving.

"I SAID GET OUT OF MY STORE, YOU FUCKING PIECE OF SHIT!!" the proprietor shouts again at the customer, and at this sixth reference to fucking shit pieces, I decide I need to remove myself from their proximity. But leaving the store would require me to elbow past the shouter and shoutee, which doesn't strike me as wise. I am not sure whether this scene is about to erupt into violence, and I have no interest in getting killed by crossfire at this stage of my life. So instead, I bolt straight to the back of the store and hide among the foam plates and toothpicks.

"YOU FUCKING PIECE OF SHIT, GET OUT OF MY STORE, YOU FUCKING PIECE OF SHIT," I hear again. The man needs a thesaurus. You'd think he could shake things up with an ASSHOLE or two, but no.

I ponder calling 911. At what point should I do so? Before or after an altercation begins? Preferably before—we'd all be better off if love and gentleness reigned through the land, or at least the dollar store—but I don't want to incur the wrath of Mr. Fucking Shit Pieces. On the other hand, if I wait until a fight breaks out, someone might wind up hurt. Or even dead. And that is untenable.

There are two other men hovering in the store, and I consider them. Will one of them call? Or intervene, maybe? No, I think. Of course they won't. No one calls or intervenes. That was the lesson of Kitty Genovese, the Queens woman murdered before her neighbors' eyes in 1964. Dan told me about that one, in a criminal law class he used to teach at Wykeham. The fact that this has even crossed my mind gives me pause. I must do something about this shouting match, I decide. As soon as possible. Before things get out of hand. And I know what this something should be.

But first, I must select a cheapo frame from this lovely selection over here by the mechanical pencils.

"YOU FUCKING FUCKING PIECE OF FUCKING SHIT! YOU PIECE OF SHIT!"

There. Poy-fect. Frame selection complete. And now, on to my civic and Christian duty.

I shuffle over toward the cleaning-fluid aisle. There I have a clear view of the front of the shop, where Mr. Fucking Shit Pieces is still maxing out his vocabulary at the intractable young man, who is now standing at the door and hurling obscenities back. They are inching closer to each other. The tension and volume are ramping up. It's time for New Amy's Mouth to make its move. I poke my head out.

HEY, MAN! JUST LEAVE!

This is me. I yell this at the non-budging customer.

JUST GET OUT OF HERE, OK?! GET OUT OF HERE!!

He looks over, temporarily thrown by this unexpected intrusion from an outside presence, especially an outside female presence pushing fifty in the household products aisle. Mr. Fucking Shit Pieces, ignoring me, continues his rant. My Loud Mouth screams right through him.

WALK AWAY! IT DOESN'T MATTER WHO'S RIGHT AT THIS POINT! DO US ALL A FAVOR, MAN! GO!

The customer stares. This is the second time I've referred to him as "Man." I idly wonder why. (*Mouth? Hello, can you hear me, Mouth? What motivates you?*) Maybe I'm reliving all those hours logged watching *Room 222* as a child.

GO! GO! I repeat, and this time, I make a shoo-shooing motion with my hands, which, like the limb of the pothead teen, have suddenly turned as autonomous as my Mouth.

"FUCKING FUCKING FUCKING PIECE OF SHIT," opines the proprietor. But the piece of shit ain't moving.

Things are getting serious, I think. It's time for my deathblow. My coup de grâce. My clincher. New Amy and Her Sovereign Mouth again spring into action.

GOD LOVES YOU!!!

I shout this. And for a moment, Mr. Fucking Shit Pieces stops his harangue.

The young man gives me a wide smile, bewildered and off his guard. He can't believe what he just heard. I can't believe that I just said it. (*Are you serious, Mouth?*) For a second or two, our shared disbelief unites us across the dollar store aisle. Apparently, no one expects a woman of a certain age to start proselytizing in the midst of a quickly escalating urban fracas. Especially the woman. Even if she's a widow. And once considered joining a convent. And stopped shaving her legs for a while. Even then.

NOW GET OUT OF HERE, MAN!! the Mouth yells one last time, wedging in one last "Man" and a few more shooing motions. Wonder of wonders, he takes my advice and leaves.

Clutching my cheap plastic frame, I emerge from my spot beside the bleach and glass cleaner. Mr. Fucking Shit Pieces rings me up at the counter, venting.

"He was so rude! And he told me *I* was rude! But *he* was rude! He opened the bag of chips before I handed him his change!"

Inwardly I say: Waiiiiit a second. This about *potato chips*? Are you *serious*, Mr. Fucking Shit Pieces??

Outwardly I say: Hunh.

"So rude," he says again. To illustrate the point, he picks up the criminal bag of chips—which the young man left behind in the kerfuffle.

But guess what, my people! It isn't even a bag of chips! It's a bag of bugles! Which are gross! And hateful! And definitely *not worth dying for*! These two dimwits almost came to blows OVER A BAG OF CORN BUGLES!

Mr. Fucking Shit Pieces hands me my change. Gives me a pained grin. Says something about having a nice day.

And *you* have a *peaceful* day, I reply.

The Mouth smiles and leaves.

39 At Rainbow Narrows

With pain and love on my mind, I drive north to Onchiota.

I'm feeling muddled. A tough exchange with a cherished friend left me hurting a few days ago, and the sting of it lingers. I think about the *bluntissimo* things I said in reply, the complicated feelings I expressed, how much hurt I delivered in return. I wonder about my skinlessness, my mood swings, my grief. Everything wounds me more than it should, and I'm tired of it. Tired of being fragile. Folks are still telling me I'm strong, but no, sorry, beg to differ, I'm not. I'm broken and I know it, aware of every shattered, scattered piece, unsure how to gather and glue myself back together. Maybe this awareness looks like strength to others. Maybe I'm just especially good at faking it. Maybe faking it is the only thing to do.

So I drive north, Mitchell in the back. Madeleine will meet us there tomorrow. Jeanne is staying home: She preferred to rest and hang with friends this weekend, so I've given her a pass. I often give the kids a pass nowadays, and why not? If someone decided to give me one, I'd take it.

My aunt and uncle live on a hill above water in a leafy, luscious pocket of the Adirondacks, off a dirt road north of Saranac Lake. They moved up there full time, to this speck on the map called Onchiota, in their seventies. Now Uncle Allie is ninety-two, and Aunt Charlotte is eighty-seven, and each time I see them, I try to capture and bottle my fragments of time with them for recollection later, whenever that later might be. They are hardy, and loving, and precise about things. Charlotte has only a few strands of gray in her dark hair. Allie went white at thirty; it's his side of the family, my mother's side, I have to blame for my silver.

At Allie and Charlotte's, I catch up with my cousin, Karen, who lost her husband two and a half years ago, and her sweet, strawberry-haired twenty-five-year-old, Travis. On Saturday, we fish off the dock down the hill on Rainbow Narrows, casting against the breeze, and talk about the strangest foods we've ever eaten. Mine was haggis—sheep's organs cooked inside a stomach. Mitchell ate an ant once, out of curiosity. I mention my friend Bob, the giant laugher, who ate plates of them on a trip down the Amazon. Travis, his kind, ruddy face lit with enthusiasm, trumps us all: He's eaten fried mealworms, which he loved. And boiled silkworm pupae, which he hated. And live octopus, which he bought from a street vendor in South Korea.

Live octopus? Not just raw?

"Live," he confirms. "It was a challenge. The vendor chops it right there, and hands it to you, and the pieces are still wriggling. As you chew them, they get stuck to your tongue and the inside of your mouth. Because of the suction cups."

Wow. A challenge, indeed. Sheep's innards do not compare.

In a bit, Travis decides we should try fishing for pike at a spot past the Narrows, on Rainbow Lake proper. So he ferries us over in a little motorboat, sitting Mitchell beside him. Does Mitchell want to try his hand at steering? He does. Travis gives him quick instruction: Squeeze this to accelerate, move this to turn. From my seat in the bow I face the lake ahead of us, the tangled knots of brush along the edge, the imposing, piney bulk of Loon Lake Mountain beyond. I smile into the wind, remembering all the many hours I spent on this water with Chris. I remember swimming out, way out, on another breezy sunny day many years ago, and stopping in the middle to tread water and dwell upon my late sister, and father, and mother. I'm good at treading water. Having grown up on a lake, I can stay afloat for hours, literally hours, and to me it's never felt like wasted time. I like holding still to think. On that day years ago, I held still, studied the light as it bounced off endless wiggling tiny crests and thought about the unity and diversity of creation, the mystery of all that braids us together while it tears us apart. I felt yoked to the past and the future, the living and the dead, the love and the grief, in a way that seemed both fleeting and eternal.

I believe in God; I believe in love; I believe they're the same thing; I believe we're made of it, breathe it, swim through it. But the older I get, the more I believe that nothing about life in this mysterious webbing is easy, nor is it meant to be. It's meant to be beautiful. It's meant to be rich. It's also meant to be painful. Why, I have no idea. But if we can accept loss, anguish, death as not merely inevitable, but imperative—as somehow necessary, like a dark thread that binds the fabric—then it becomes part of the beauty, the joy, even, of this transcendental bustle we call living. Treading water that day, I felt connected. To my love, my grief, my family in the next world, my family in this one. To my unseen future, and my half-remembered past. To all of it.

I think of this now, heading out in search of pike. I think of Chris, and I recall something a friend said a couple weeks back, quoting Jane Hirshfield's seven-word reduction of Zen Buddhism: "Everything changes. Everything is connected. Pay attention." It's then that I turn around—and I see Mitchell, his hand on the engine, his hair whipped back in the wind, his huge grin crammed with braces, and the unexpected, inexpressible bliss of ripping along the water in a motor boat. He's paying attention. And in that moment, so am I.

We return pike-less. Later in the day, Travis takes us out in the boat once more—to a rope swing just across the Narrows. Karen joins us. The swing drapes thirty feet from a haggard-looking pine that tilts forward at an angle too acute for comfort, its roots barely clawing the fine sand at the edge. We've done this before many times, though not in a couple of years, and we're confident that the tree won't fall, the swing won't kill us. It's chilly for August, maybe 70 in the sun, and the sun's being fickle today. The water's as warm as it ever gets in these deep Adirondack lakes, which is to say, not very.

I go first. These days, I feel determined to go first. I don't know why. Mid-life machisma, possibly. A way to prove to myself that I'm alive. Fear, perhaps, that if I don't go first I'll chicken out later. New Amy doesn't chicken out.

The rope is inches thick, knotted, frayed. It scratches my forearms. I carry it up the incline to a pair of rocks jammed into a makeshift shelf, then step up and grab the third knot. I hoist myself, kick up my legs and soar down the hill, over the water, into the sky. I release myself into the blue. I spin. I howl. I splash down, taking a schnozz full of water, and swim up into the air again, smiling. Awesome.

Over and over I do this, taking my turn with the others. After the seventh or eighth time, my overtaxed arms begin to complain, groaning loudly that they aren't well-equipped to bear my weight. So I sit on the hill with Karen, and for a time we watch our two fatherless boys propel themselves through the air. Travis writhes and whirls and slams, displacing major tonnage. Mitchell, compact and athletic, tucks himself into a ball and hangs in the air for a split-second that seems like eternity, then drops like a bomb straight down. Little moments like this ripple forever. Are forever. Will be forever. Just because they're over doesn't mean they're gone. As Faulkner once wrote, "The past is never dead. It's not even past."

I think back on the pain and love that underscored my drive to Onchiota, the pain and love that underscore my grief at losing Chris. It's all one piece. It occupies time but lies somehow beyond it, a quantity unmeasured on an earthly scale but there, always felt, always known. Love is pain and pain is love, and the only surefire way to avoid the one is to forego the other—a well-duh axiom if there ever was one. I've figured that much out. I and everyone else who ever lived.

Karen and I talk about our losses. We talk about the everyday strangeness of downsizing, accommodating, making our way without our husbands. We talk about our faith and our fear of being alone. We talk about how hard it is to see older couples hand in hand. We talk about our lawns: Karen, too, had her struggles with a way-too-heavy mower. We talk about the need to reinvent and redefine ourselves. Later on, in the kitchen at dusk, we talk about how direct we've become, how honest, how impatient we've become with the dishonesty and immaturity of others. We talk about dating (not yet, but someday) and men's irrational fear of widows.

And sitting on the bank at Rainbow Narrows, on a brisk Adirondack afternoon, we talk about letting go. We agree that there's no way forward unless we surrender up the past, giving it over—with all of its guilt, regrets, unspoken words, and unrealized dreams—to the incomprehensible vastness of life and love that both of us know as God.

I gesture to Mitchell and Travis, still launching themselves into the firmament.

That's letting go, I say. Right there.

Karen laughs in agreement.

I'm going off again, I say. One more swing. My arms are killing me, but just one more swing.

And so I get up and grab the rope, its fibers scratching the raw red insides of my forearms. My biceps are screaming. They can't believe I'm about to do this again. When I pull my weight once more, the arms almost fail me, and my heels drag in the sand on my descent. At last I yank up my legs and fly out, up, out, hitting the apex in an instant so brief I'm sure I'll miss it and arc back into the tree. But I don't miss it. I don't crash. The instant lasts and lasts and lasts, and I have all the time in the world to let go. The loving sky enfolds me, and I fall.

40 Looking for Mr. Manly Pants, Part II

With or without the hitchhiker, I am lonely beyond belief. This is what I tell people who ask how I'm doing. I would describe myself as horny, but this particular qualifier would embarrass 99.9 percent of the folks I relate to on a regular basis, and while I care very little what other people think of me, I nevertheless prefer not to make them choke on their spit, or otherwise traumatize any of them so severely that they resolve never to speak to me again.

I am lonely beyond belief. The "phantom limb" pain and touch deprivation have now reached crisis levels, as has my overall yearning for a new Mr. Manly Pants to hold me and spoon with me and do other worthwhile and interesting things to me and, of course, leave his revolting beard shavings in the sink. I need all of this. And I need it soon.

Various friends have suggested, wisely, kindly, that maybe this might take a while, that maybe I'll have to be a little patient before I find my next good man, and, OK, yes, OK, OK, they're right. From an outsider's viewpoint, I'm in an indecent hurry. But you know what? I hurt NOW. NOW I am coping with more daily torment than I've ever known. NOW I am suffering from a complete loss of intimacy. NOW I crave a pair of arms stronger and hairier than my own. I want someone to soothe me, love me, be with me, laugh with me, breath on me and watch crappy TV with me NOW. Got that? NOOOOWWWWW. Me. Lonely. Now.

Unfortunately, I have no idea how to go about this. I haven't been on the market in twenty-two years, and I was never any good at dating, anyway. The field of available men-folk somewhere near my age has waned dramatically in the ensuing decades; as Jane so aptly puts it (she and I often commiserate on this subject), almost every guy we know is married, gay, or dead. Presumably, some single, straight, live cutie between the ages of forty-six and sixty-two is hiding behind an arborvitae somewhere nearby, but if so, I've yet to find him.

Ring scans have become habitual. But they aren't totally reliable, because any given ringless man might be gay, married, dating someone, married and dating someone, or allergic to metal. At Tamar's suggestion I've started tossing the loneliness bomb into casual conversation with people I know, as in, "Hey, thanks for asking, the kids and I are doing swell, but did I mention my libido's been on fire lately and, by the way, do you happen to know any available single sort-of-normal non-sociopathic men over the age of fifty? Ha ha ha ha ha only joking? Except I'm not? I'm sorry, are you asphyxiated right now, and does that mean our conversation has come to a close?"

The first time I do this, it doesn't go so well. My friend winds up telling me about some chick she knew whose husband died tragically, and then she went off and got married too soon, like, less than six months later, which is roughly the expiration date on bologna. Everyone seems to know some chick who married too soon, and everyone is outraged about it. I hadn't realized how common this sort of thing is until my husband died and people started regaling me with such tales of degeneracy. The message seems to be, YOU aren't treating your husband like bologna! YOU'RE grieving for the proper length of time!

What I always say when someone tells me this is:

Well, the loneliness, the loss of intimacy, is unbelievable. I can barely describe it to you. It's an unbearable physical pain. I wouldn't judge anyone who started dating immediately and got married immediately after.

What they always say in reply is:

Oh, of course! The loneliness must be terrible! I can only imagine!

What I say in response is:

Seriously, I've heard stories of widows who go around picking up guys at bars.

And they say:

Oh, of course! I can only imagine!

And I say:

At least I'm not picking up guys at bars.

And they say:

Oh, of course not! Ha ha ha ha ha!

And I say:

Of course not! Ha ha ha ha ha!

And the conversation winds up at more or less the same place where it began, i.e., with me in a state of frustrating and seemingly permanent manlessness. What to do?

Match.com is a possibility. A friend whose husband left her advises me on it: Any guy who claims to enjoy "wine-tasting," she warns, drinks like a fish. A guy who doesn't drink at all is a recovering alcoholic (fine by me). Always meet a guy in a public place for lunch, she stresses. And remember, there are a lot of weirdos out there. But don't let that stop you.

Eeek.

My niece, who found her boyfriend on Match, lectures me about the proper method. This takes her half an hour. She is a dear thing, full of generosity and enthusiasm, and she wants me to find someone to cure my loneliness. I keep saying thank you, but I'm not there yet, I'm not there yet, and she keeps saying, "Amy, you have too much life in you not to do this." She is a doll for saying so. But I am not going the Match.com route. I've seen some of those profiles, and the guys adopt names like Loverrr4U and NmerrUnoHunk, which I don't find particularly attractive but have the advantageous temporary side effect of killing my sex drive.

Also: Would I really be willing to post my photo? After .3 milliseconds of deliberation, I decide I wouldn't. I don't want people recognizing me online and then bumping into me at the grocery store, saying, Hey, Girlfree-und! I saw your pic on Match.com!

And I was never secure about my looks, even in my twenties. Now I have gray hair and wrinkles.

Eeek.

Another friend of mine says she tried eHarmony.com, which uses a super-duper-deep questionnaire and fancy algorithm to align people emotionally and spiritually. She wouldn't recommend it, as it kept matching her up with "guitar-playing mailmen from Minnesota," but if some dude in short pants showed up at my doorstep with a twelve-string and my electric bill, and started belting out "In Your Eyes" in a Great Lakes accent with something close to accurate pitch, I would not kick him down the stoop.

So, one night, desperately, fuckingly lonely (and yes, since my husband died, "fuckingly" has become a proper English adverb), I register for eHarmony.com. I do this without telling anyone except Pam, who's all for it. I do this whilst thinking I must be out of my silver-haired proverbial head. I do this without actually believing I'll find someone. But I do this anyway.

Eeek.

No guitar-playing mailmen for me. No, instead I'm paired with patriotic Christian Gold Wing fanatics from West Virginia.

Gold Wings are motorcycles, the cushy touring kind one sees in the slow lane laden with several packs and two zaftig people, and you'd be surprised to learn how many men upload photos of them to dating websites. You'd also be surprised to learn how many of these same men list Fox News as a cause for gratitude.

At first, I am not sure why I'm being set up with these ultra-right-wing recreational biker types, as I made my liberal politics perfectly clear on my initial questionnaire. But I also indicated my open-mindedness and OKness with dating anyone of any background or belief system. If eHarmony decided to set me up with some warm and adorable atheist, that would be A-OK, peeps. B'hai? Muslim? Buddhist? I don't care. Bring on the Shinto hotties!

But then I realize: I had revealed, in several places, my own devout Christianity. And I suspect there is a large population of lefties, atheists, and practitioners of other religions who would automatically eliminate anyone who claims to be a devout Christian — precisely because of the patriotic Fox News-watching Gold Wing contingent. At the same time, there is likely a sizeable chunk of the patriotic Fox News-watching Gold Wing contingent that *only* wants to be paired with a devout Christian woman.

Which I am. And because I indicated on my questionnaire that I'm tolerant and open to dating anyone, of any political or religious belief system, I get paired with these gents. And these are the gents who, in a section of the website devoted to random stupid pointless questions, say they'd never date an atheist. Other helpful questions reveal their favorite Muppet, favorite Kardashian, feelings about chewing tobacco, opinion of people who paint their faces at sporting events and, best of all, ability to roll their tongues ("I have never tried"). Some of them, when asked if they'd date a widow, check "unsure." (Excuse me, man, but: Fuck you?!?) One guy I'm matched with admits to having been unfaithful; what sort of dumbass admits to that on eHarmony.com?

Eeek.

Here's my problem. As religious as I am, I have no desire to be with someone who wouldn't want to be with me if I *weren't* religious. I don't want to belong to any club that wouldn't have me if I didn't fit the bill; I much prefer to be with people who accept me despite my shortcomings. This is the same logic I applied when, years ago, I signed up my family with the Jewish Community Center despite the fact that we're not Jewish. They have most excellent gym facilities and a marvelous outdoor pool.

And no one gives a damn that we don't qualify. So we swim with the Jews.

With this in mind, I go into the "background and beliefs" page on eHarmony and see about toning down the religiosity component of my profile. Aside from denying up front that I'm Christian (should I click "other"?), there is no clear way to do this—and no way to opt out of the belief component altogether. It's simply not allowed. You have to own up to your beliefs or claim to have none at all, you damned fool heathen! Which I am tempted to do. Because, as a matter of fact, damned fool heathens! are among the loveliest people I know. But it would make me a liar. Which I have claimed not to be in another portion of my profile. Which is really starting to piss me off.

In a desperate move, I slide the cursor over to the section slugged "Please indicate what religion(s) your matches should be affiliated with (check all that apply)" and uncheck the box that says "no preference." Instead, I methodically check off everything but "Christian." Surely this makes me an apostate. Surely this relegates me to some inner circle of Dante's hell, rubbing elbows with all those miserable bloody heretics in flaming tombs. But there is no other way to eliminate the annoying subset of devout Christians who automatically write off everyone but *other* devout Christians.

And so I eliminate the entire blessed category. I deep-six my fellow followers of Christ, every last one of them. This wasn't exactly the point of registering with eHarmony.com, which promised to hook me up with a spiritually compatible piece of man-meat. Right? RIGHT?

I click "Save." I head over to the "My Matches" page. I click on "Find New Matches."

I wait a minute while the super-duper-deep vetting process searches for exciting new prospects. Dum-dee-dum-dum. La-la-la.

I wait some more. It finds no one.

Eeek.

41 Things I Can't Say to Your Face, Part IV

Time doesn't pass where you are, but it makes a good show of passing here. Or not. Most days it seems to sit, its haunches plopped directly on my lap so I can't move. I often feel pinned by its motionless heft. And yet, the two of us together, I and this pressing accumulation of time, have apparently plodded forward through most of a year. I am not sure how. I am not sure why. I am not sure that either of us, at this point, can do any more significant plodding. But I know that the next minute will come, and the next hour, and the next day, and week, and month, and year, and soon enough the plodding will have brought me along to my own death. Where I will, at last, face you again.

In the meantime, I drive Madeleine to Georgetown. I also drive all of her stuff. Back when my mother and sister drove me off to Hamilton, I packed some clothes, a milk crate or two, my favorite pillow, a mustard-colored manual typewriter, and exactly four pairs of shoes: running shoes, soccer cleats, winter boots, and a pair of those little Chinese cotton maryjanes that everyone wore in the 80s. Our beautiful eldest daughter packs an entire bin of footwear.

I observe it in the living room. I observe many things in the living room, because Madeleine's bedroom has puked its contents all over the first floor. Among the many many bins holding many many objects for her many many needs at Georgetown is one holding approximately 8,281 pairs of shoes.

I regard it. Madeleine regards me regarding it. Then I say: Honey, that's a whole lot of shoes.

She says something in urgent tones indicating that all of them are necessary.

I say: Really? You need them all?

She says something once again, in even more urgent tones, indicating that all of them are necessary.

I say: Remember, we're taking the Matrix to Georgetown. It is not a large car. In fact, it is a small car. And besides all of your stuff, we have to pack you into it. And your brother and sister. And me.

This is where I begin to make myself really popular. Because, for the next three days, Madeleine periodically comes up to me with some new, roughly-80-gallon plastic bin of Totally Totally Necessary Shit. And blurts the following question: "Mom. How do you think I should pack this?"

Whereupon Mom says:

You might have to leave it behind.

Whereupon Madeleine says:

"Mom! I just want to know how I should pack this!"

Whereupon Mom says:

You might have to leave it behind.

Whereupon Madeleine says:

"MOM!! MOM!! PLEASE STOP TELLING ME I'LL HAVE TO LEAVE EVERYTHING BEHIND, AND JUST GIVE ME SOME ADVICE!! JUST TELL ME HOW TO PACK THIS!!"

Whereupon Mom says something along the lines of:

I am the voice of doom! You must leave your shit behind! Bwahahahahahaha!

Which, as I reflect on it now, isn't all that helpful. To the contrary, it's remarkably lazy and unhelpful; I was only trying to side-step some of the gruntwork in Madeleine's college-packing F.S.O. And Madeleine, practiced in the art and craft of being my daughter, ignores this remarkably lazy and unhelpful advice and continues to pack up her belongings for insertion into our adorable Japanese compact. And I order a mondo soft waterproof roof carrier from Amazon.com, an item, when it arrives, that promises the capacity of the Lincoln Tunnel. I am hopeful that, through some mystical college-packing-young-person Feng Shui, we will somehow haul four people + Madeleine's worldly goods ~400 miles down the Eastern seaboard.

Still, when I talk to Pam the Thursday before we leave, she expresses doubt. She suggests I might want to borrow someone's van. She suggests I might want to rent something larger from U-Haul. She suggests that maybe I might want to get a commercial driver's license and then employ Jiu-Jitsu to beat down a trucker and hijack his 18-wheeled Kenworth semi for the move, and while she doesn't say this out loud, I know that's what she's thinking.

What she says out loud is: "I keep picturing Mitchell with a snorkel."

What I say out loud is: Hahahaha! That's right! The car will be packed so tight, the kids will need breathing tubes! Hahahaha!

What I don't say out loud is: SHIT! Maybe Pam's right. Snorkeling equipment. Where could I buy that? Dick's?

And yet, by some miracle, without assistance from her remarkably lazy and unhelpful mother, Madeleine squishes everything into the car and the rooftop carrier, leaving room between the shoes for four actual human beings. Before we pull out of the driveway, we say a prayer. Please God, give us a safe trip. Please God, may we not break down. Please God, help Madeleine settle into Georgetown. Please God, bless Dad in heaven.

I put the car in gear. Madeleine smiles. "There isn't room in here for Dad, anyway," she observes, and we all crack up. Thank the Lord for black humor. Thank the Lord for our children, who are more together than I am.

The trip to D.C. goes on forever and ever, requiring lengthy pee stops every 4.3 minutes, but we arrive. We stay with your sister, Marie, and her husband, Michael, the two of them as lovely and welcoming as ever. They miss you. We all do. The word "miss" does not convey the protracted surrealism of moving through this world without you. All these months later, you should be here. You should be now. You should be helping your daughter unpack her flip-flops in a third-floor freshman dorm room at your alma mater, where your absence is present at every turn.

I try to keep a lid on my emotions, but they leak out, and the kids notice. They notice everything about me these days. I tell them I'm sorry, I tell them I'm fine, I tell them Dad is here with us—they know that, right? They say they do. Perhaps they do. I'm not sure myself. I'm not sure whether you're with us as we hoof back and forth across this proud and verdant campus, or whether you're off in the netherworld doing something vastly more important. The chores of this world occupy us so, demand so much of our sweat and attention, that we think less on the abstract business of the next one. And few things require more sweat and attention than moving a child into the next daunting chapter of her life.

So I give up trying to imagine your spirit beside us. Instead, I try to find a simulacrum of you here, in the flesh, in some first-year student processing up the aisle at Convocation. You're hard to find. I search first each young man's face, looking for that bright spark of erudition, curiosity, and humor. I look for the ramrod posture, so straight it nearly tilts back. I look for the tight swimmer's frame and small stature, knowing you grew three inches in college and acquired muscle later. I look for a frizz of wiry brown hair that soon became a 'fro. I look for blue eyes, or maybe gray, or maybe a blend with green. I look for confidence.

Youths file past me. Boys who believe they're men already: towering basketball players, burly preps in button-down shirts the color of melon. Latinos and Asians and African-Americans and everyone else, from everywhere else, all of them in khaki. Nerds traveling in packs, swapping ironic glances. Nerds traveling alone, looking lonely and hesitant and soft. What seems to be an entire freshman rugby team, necks thick and hair mussed. A hipster in pastel with architect glasses.

One young man reminds me of you: He has the look of a lively Irish sprig. But he slouches. I spot another one—on the short side, neither cocky nor shy, neither dorky nor jockish, light on his feet despite the heft of his brain. He glances in my direction. Maybe. Maybe it's you. The hair not frizzy enough, the eyes too dark—but a glint in them. And skinnier, for sure, but weren't you, back then? There's a sweetness, a funniness. A readiness to laugh.

And then I see her: Madeleine in a white cotton dress. I was searching for her all along. She's beautiful. She's beaming. And I understand that she's not mine, but ours, still ours, never less than ours—even now, with me here and you there, wherever *there* is.

In your absence, you're with me, somehow. With all of us, bound by the loving essence of who you were and whatever, however, you are now. One day I'll find you and hold you again, whether we embrace with our arms or something better. But for now, I find and hold you in our children, whom we made with our love, through God's love, and sent into life on earth with an almighty love that never ends. And so I know that you don't, either.

42 My Homie, Job

"It's like Job."

Pam says this, but I don't mean to single her out (I love her to pieces). She isn't the only one. Many people say it. The people who don't say it think it. The people who don't think it would think it if they gave it half a sec, and then they'd wonder why it hadn't occurred to them before. Comparisons with the afflicted *pater familias* of the ancient Israelites are too obvious to dodge, and I can understand why. Chris's psychiatric tailspin and his suicide six months later suggest a run of biblically bum luck, if not evidence that God and his adversary sometimes amuse themselves with grotesque celestial parlor games. ("Wanna bet, God? Watch me drive her husband crazy and make him leap to his death, and THEN she'll curse you! Ha ha ha! Just wait!")

But I resist being likened to Job: My kids are still sound of mind and body, and hallelujah for that. My job remains my job. My five-hundred yoke of oxen are still alive, or they would be if I had any, and my 7,000 imaginary sheep are yet to be incinerated by holy fire raining from heaven. I am not covered in excruciating boils. So far, my friends haven't parked themselves at my feet for a week and lectured me about my sins.

I'm not Job. No way am I Job. I might be a shit magnet, but I'm not Job! Or any feminine variation on same! Whatever that would be! (Jobette? Jobie-Sue?)

When I found the lump in my breast, I had a moment of doubt. Then it turned out to be nothing, or at any rate, an unscary something, and I returned to my feelings of Job-less-ness. Here I remained. Right, so my husband was still dead, and

my children were still fatherless, and I was still working a job
that most newspapers have eliminated in a time of constant and
widespread downsizing. I was still at the mercy of the Incredible
Shrinking Industry. But I had my health. I had my children. I
had my house. I had an amazing network of support. I'd just
bought a new car, my Matrix, and I had the M&M photo to
prove it. Yay. I had my cat. I had my health insurance. Hurray. I
still had that job. All good.

Then the Matrix drifted into a guard rail in the middle of a
$%*(!@# snowstorm on the drive home from my parents' house
in Vermont. The @!!#$ thing was only going ten miles per hour,
but that didn't prevent it from sustaining $5,000 in $#@!!
damage. My $&!!@# insurance rates went up. When I told my
dad, he made some crack about shit magnets.

Ha ha ha! I responded. That's right! That is SO funny. Yet
more proof that I'm a shit magnet! Ha ha ha ha ha!

I said this, not pausing to consider that Job was the shit
magnet to end all shit magnets. In the annals of shit magnetism,
there is no greater exemplar than Job. No magnet before or since
has attracted that much shit, that fast, with that much play-by-
play commentary, and then found himself the subject of a best-
selling book. Why, he practically invented shit!

Which is, I guess, one more reason I'm not Job. The shit I
attract is NOTHING like the shit he attracted.

This I tell myself, over and over. Even when the cat runs
away: Oliver, a quirky twelve-year-old black-and-white
shorthair. Oliver, a dog in a cat's body. Oliver, who took to
sleeping on my knees after Chris died. Oliver, the closest thing I
have to oxen.

The kids are distraught. He'll come back, I tell them. Just
watch. Our luck will turn. He'll come back.

He doesn't come back.

Then I lose my health insurance. I continue it through
Cobra. Once a month, I detach one of my limbs and mail it as
payment to the insurance company. Eventually I will run out of

arms and legs, which (ironically) may require some medical help down the line, but for now: a solution.

When folks aren't calling me Job, they're comparing me to victims of war. I am not a victim of war. My mother, my father, my sister, and my husband might be dead, my breasts might be lumpy, my all-weather radials might be ineffective, my cat might be missing, my insurance might have vanished, and my facial orifices might be discharging non-stop saline, but I am otherwise in halfway decent shape. I still have my kids. I still have my family and friends. I still have my paycheck.

I am *so* not Job.

I pick up the bible and dip into his story, so agonizing, so poetic. As ever, it baffles me. I connect with his grief ("my inward parts seethe and will not be stilled") and his pleas for an explanation ("let the Almighty answer me!"), but I have a hard time reconciling my loving Creator with the wuss who's bullied into torturing a decent and faithful man. Man up, God! I never understood how the author of Job came to devise this scenario (no, I don't regard it as an accurate journalistic account of an historical event), and I never understood the point of Job's prolonged beatdown. It's not as though Job begins as an arrogant douche who *needs* to be humbled. He's humble at the start. When God blows in at the close and lectures him about thunderstorms, and Leviathans, and being stronger and wiser and cooler than anyone could possibly imagine, this isn't new information to Job. Job never doubted God. Job is one of the good guys.

All right, so bad stuff happens to good people. Yeah? And? THE POINT BEING? The point being that bad stuff happens to good people. *Really* bad stuff happens to *really* good people. What's more, monumentally shitty stuff happens to unbelievably saintly people. Bad stuff/good people/bad stuff/good people, over and over again. Department of Redundancy Department. This is what my friends mean when they compare me to Job. I am good. The shit is bad. I did nothing to deserve it. Right.

Each time I flip it open, this is all I get from Job. And then I flip it shut.

One Wednesday night, our friends, Fred and Diana, at the Albany Catholic Worker host a Mass and potluck in memory of Chris, who gave generously of himself with time and carpentry. It's a warm, lovely, loving evening with good friends who include two priests: Father Bob from Chris's wake, Father Chris from the funeral. The Mass is held in a crowded basement room, where we sit in a circle and listen to the night's difficult scripture passages—that business in the Gospel about plucking out an eye that causes you to sin. Nice one. And for the Old Testament reading, Job. At the homily we all share stories of Chris's life, the good works he did, the restful Sundays he observed, our restless sorrow in the long months since. I talk about the mystery of love and loss and joy and pain, everything twined together, and my sense that I'm connected—somehow—to a divine mysterious fabric that covers all of it.

At the Peace, Father Chris holds onto me a moment longer. "We have to talk about Job," he says with a smile.

I think: Oh, nooooo. Not Job again. YOU TOO, FATHER CHRIS?

But this is not what I say aloud, because I love Father Chris, I trust Father Chris, I want to be nice to Father Chris, and I am happy to talk to Father Chris at any time about anything. Even the Totally Befuddling Book of Job. And who knows? Maybe he'll de-fuddle it for me. So instead I say:

Job! Of course! Ha ha! Yes! OK!

"I have some insights. I read a book that changed my entire understanding of it. So let's get together."

I've dipped into the Book of Job since Chris died, I say. And there's some comfort there. But it's baffling.

"This'll change your way of looking at it."

OK.

As promised, we get together a week later and talk Job for a solid hour. Father Chris, inspired by Jack Miles's *God: A Biography*, explains for me the true meaning of Job. I grok its totality. It turns out I'm baffled by the Book of Job because, wouldn't you know it, the Book of Job is baffling! Because God is baffling! The whole book concerns the babbling bafflement of the believer, a logical reaction when faced with the paradox of a powerful and merciful God, who either dishes shit out—or just sits on his hands as shit gets dished out, lots of shit, and does nothing to stop it. What's *that* about? And then, just to be irritating, he refuses to explain why! What's generally read as acquiescence on Job's part (at the very end, when he repents) is a simple human matter of the poor man throwing up his hands and saying: All right already, Mr. All-Powerful God Person! Get out of my face! You make no sense to me and never will! You're never going to answer my question, anyway! So I take it all back! Leave me alone! Blah blah blah!

In other words, I say, I'm supposed to be baffled.

Father Chris nods. "We're supposed to be baffled."

That's the only response.

"That's the only response."

Because life is baffling. The good and evil, the love and the loss. It's all life. It's all God.

"It's all God."

Hmmm.

We tug a little harder on this thought. But as Christians, he says, we don't stop at the inscrutable "power God." We keep going all the way to Jesus—to our powerless God on the cross—and to the Holy Spirit. That God is always with us, especially in the shit. That God calls us to love and be God to one another.

At the end of our conversation, Father Chris suggests we meet again to discuss more Job. "You're living it," he says.

I am? I don't think I am, I say. Or maybe I just don't want to think I am.

I head home. Digest everything. Repeat it back to friends. Consider the ramifications. Pray on it. Reflect on it for a few days. Carry it over the weekend and into the following Monday. Begin my work. Check my voice messages. Find one from my managing editor. Call her back. Get her assistant. Wait as my boss comes to the phone. Get laid off.

OK, I give up.

I'm Job.

43 Unemployment

So here I am, Ms. Modern Day Job-elina Jolie, applying for unemployment and loving every single minute of it. What fun! New shit to figure out! I've never done this before! Ha ha ha! But then, I'd never applied for Social Security before either, and that was a laff riot. This time, no one asks me about my current marital status, but I do find myself in a Kafkaesque alter-verse where three things are required of anyone who enters:

1) The readiness and willingness to look for a job;

2) The readiness and willingness to start a job at a moment's frickin' notice; and

3) The readiness and willingness to receive $$$$ from the Fed ONLY for days that involve no work whatsoever, even less than an hour's worth, even if it's unpaid or for a friend or on spec or might hypothetically lead to hypothetical money many hypothetical years into the hypothetical future. (The exact wording: "Any activity that brings in or may bring in income at any time must be reported.") So, if you want to receive any unemployment checks without getting hauled up on fraud charges, best not to spend time writing a book or inventing an intergalactic teleportation device.

I hadn't been planning any mad-scientist antics on the roof of my house, but I had hoped to get some writing done, and so this part vexes me. Also, I'm not convinced that writing classifies as an activity that "may bring in income," any more than Morris dancing or advanced Popsicle art "may bring in income." My neighbor George, who fronts his own band, is a fine one to commiserate on this subject; he agrees that in writing, like music,

"You can make *literally* hundreds of dollars!" And that's if you're lucky, people.

But I am laid off. I am a single mother of three. I AM JOB! (As I yell proudly from the rooftop, where I'm not inventing teleportation.) I need unemployment benefits. I need to NOT go to federal prison, where, being Job, I can only assume that I would contract a disease with hideous seeping boils. As a result, after discussing this with friends, I resolve to write a certain number of hours each week and then report them as work time to Uncle Sam. Hurray for F.S.O.!

Otherwise, I go through the usual unemployment rituals. I make a few phone calls, send a few emails, shake a few hands, talk to a jobs placement consultant, and worry about my resume, which hasn't yet been updated for the 21st century. Nor have I been updated for the 21st century. I need to jazz myself up. Open a Twitter account and a Pinterest account, then figure out what the hell to do with both of them. Even more shit-tastic new shit to figure out.

Jeanne helps.

JEANNE! JEANNE! HOW DO I TWEET? I scream.

"Right there from the website!" she screams back.

OK, I FOUND IT, I yell before I find it, because I don't want her to think I'm a total loser. But then I do find it—a slot in the upper left-hand corner that says, of all things, "Compose new tweet." I stick my cursor there. Try to come up with something witty to say. Feel stymied.

JEANNE! JEANNE! I scream again. WHAT SHOULD I TWEET?

"What??!!"

I SAID, WHAT SHOULD I TWEET? I HAVE NO IDEA WHAT TO TWEET! HELP ME, DAUGHTER! HELP! HELP!

Jeanne, concerned by my feebleness, hustles into the room to provide assistance. After thirty seconds of discussion, I type in: "Here I am on Twitter, trying to haul myself forcibly into the 21st century. Is it working?" The implied answer being, of course,

"No way, Lady. Go back to your dank cave with its manual typewriter, dial telephone, and black-and-white Zenith TV, because we're better off here without you." But surprisingly, no one says that. Followers (I have followers?) send kudos through the ether. They clamor for my tweets.

I wonder if Job had a Twitter account. The Bible never explains how his friends got the news about all those incinerated sheep, and while it's possible they heard via express donkey messenger, it's also possible Job understood the power of social media. So, who knows, maybe my kinship with Job extends to the internet.

In a new-millennium frame of mind, I decide to attend an open house at a multimedia marketing company that moved into a neighborhood church. So I spiff myself up in a black jacket and sparkly scarf.

How's this, Jeanne? Is this presentable? Do I look OK?

Jeanne approves, even if she finds my constant need for fashion advice somewhat hilarious.

"Mom!" she says at one point. "You'll be old, and you'll be dressing, and you'll take a photo of yourself in some outfit, and you'll send it to me, and then you'll call me up and ask" — here she adopts the voice of a gnarled old biddy — `What do you think, Jeanne? Should I wear this to Bingo Night?'"

What! You imagine me going to Bingo Night!?

"Yes," Jeanne says, and that is the end of that.

So I march myself down to the hip new media company and force myself to schmooze. When not shoving my hand out and waving my business card in people's noses, I eat as much free food as possible. Mitchell soon arrives with his pal, Ian, and Ian's mom, Carolyn, and the free food continues. Cake is involved. We wander around the converted interior, marveling at the hipness and beauty of the place; if you're going to secularize a sacred building, this is how to do it. The church's old pews have been repurposed as soaring wood panels and graceful furniture. I walk up to an employee leaning back at a desk.

I was a parishioner here! So my butt was on that table! Ha ha ha!

The young man glances up and grins politely. It seems he finds the mental image less amusing than I do.

I find myself in a bit of an altered state, noshing and gassing with hipsters in this church where Chris and the kids and I worshipped as a family of five. I'm both the Old Amy who prayed here and the New Amy who eats and cracks jokes about her buttocks. Once again, as I did when I first returned to work, I feel as though I'm occupying parallel bodies in parallel universes: I'm a character in a sci-fi saga, my reality shot and splintered among dimensions while some overactive orchestral score explodes with horns beneath me.

Maybe this is everyone's reality. Life gets advertised as a tidy linear narrative, but it's not; its subplots are many and timeless, the connections between them profound. We don't live just one life. We live many. I've had my life in the womb, my life with my late parents and sister at a lake in Connecticut, my life as a single and striving twentysomething, my life as a Catholic wife and mother of three. I'm still that mother; I'm still that Catholic; I'm everything I ever was, and yet I'm not. I'm changed. All of us are. Gone is our life as a unit of five, and so are our spots in the pews.

An enormous screen hovers above what used to be the altar, the holy niche where Catholics believe the bread and wine become the body and blood of Jesus. Change is always a tough one to swallow, but no change is harder to swallow than transubstantiation. It's the ultimate about-face, this metamorphosis from unadorned foodstuffs into God incarnate. Somehow, this realization makes all the many alterations—to the altar, the church, my life—easier to accept. Everything changes. Everything is connected. Pay attention.

At home that night, I say a few prayers with Mitchell. He offers this one: "May the bad stuff roll out, and the good stuff come in."

And once more I say, amen.

44 The Wisdom of the Pam

"Job's story doesn't end there."

Pam again. In an email, this time.

She has a way with words. Wise. Calm. Economical in thought and expression. Early on in my noodle-headed quest to replace the Old Amy with some devil-may-care, party-animal Newish Amy, she suggested that I might want to go small in my efforts at rebellion. "Start with jaywalking," she said.

The evening after the funeral, she was on my front steps when a dog and its owner ambled past. Holding a baggie full of poop, the owner mumbled a question Pam couldn't quite hear, but being a friendly soul, she nodded. And the dog-walker, taking this as assent, dumped the bag of feces into my trash can. "So you see? You really *are* a shit magnet," she informed me later, prompting my heartiest laugh of the day.

Back in college, when the two of us played soccer, Pam had a wizard-like ability to place herself on the field exactly where she needed to be at any given time — without actually moving to get there. I don't know how she did it. I never saw her run. Maybe Scotty beamed her over from the transporter room of the *Enterprise*. But she was the only midfielder I've ever known who could power the ball fifty yards with either foot and then instantaneously zap herself to the other end for a quick assist to some piteous and struggling forward (generally me). She always had my back. She always knew where to be, how to get there, and what to do to help. She still does.

And so, addressing my layoff, she knows without a moment's hesitation what to say. She reminds me that Job, after losing everything—including his hissy fit with God—then goes on to a second act brimming with joy and prosperity.

Thus sayeth Pam.

I flip back to Job. I turn to that wee bit at the end where Job becomes obscenely rich. It says it right there: His wealth balloons to 14,000 sheep, 6,000 thousand camels, 1,000 yoke of oxen, and 1,000 she-asses. In addition, he goes on to father ten more children (I'd like to hear from his wife) and lives another 140 years. For the record, and I'm saying this to anyone who's listening, including God, I do not want to live another 140 years. Forty would be more than enough, for me. Fifty would be tolerable with my wits, my health, and a small circle of surviving loved ones. Anything beyond that is undesirable and inconceivable, unless I'm outfitted with stem-to-stern bionic replacement parts and a chip at the base of my skull that streams Netflix directly into my visual cortex.

But I get the point. Pam wants me to remember that Job doesn't die miserable. Against all odds, after attracting all that shit, his luck turns, the shit stops, he gets happy. Could that happen to me someday? What about *my* second act? Will I have she-asses, too?

It's a nice thought, but I'm skeptical of this nifty footnote to the Job story; it's pat. It seems to me, after my exegesis with Father Chris, that Job's efforts at F.S.O. don't take him anywhere concrete, leading him deeper and deeper down winding subterranean passageways to nowhere. All that he knows is that he knows nothing, that God is unfathomable, that life is at best a dicey prospect—so what's the point of even trying to figure it out, bro? The point is that it's un-figure-out-able. All of it. The bad, the good, the God. So that happy-peppy payoff at the end, where Job gets Door Number Three (the All-Expense-Paid Trip to Fiji, Plus a New Car, and Really Cute Sheep!), strikes me as far too mawkish and obvious. I'm pretty sure that if the Book of Job were released as a mega-budgeted summer movie with lots of gratuitous explosions, and I hadn't been laid off, and I got assigned to review it, and I was in a cranky mood, I would have ripped the thing to shreds for the sappiness of its postscript. It's just too *neat*. Few things ever galled me more than a film that betrayed itself with some cheap maneuver at the end.

But Pam has me wondering. It's possible, I suppose, that the unfathomability of God and life applies across the board. Joy can rain down upon us as inexplicably as misery — on Job, or anyone. No one demands an explanation of the Almighty when the good shit hits the fan. No one screeches, "WHY, GOD, WHY?" when the dream job comes knocking, when true love appears out of nowhere, when a healthy child is born with ten fingers, ten toes, and a dimple. We just accept these things as a matter of course — and maybe say thanks, if we remember. But they're just as outrageous and capricious and illogical and mysterious and unlikely and unearned and *unfair* as Job's own trials. So the Wisdom of the Pam gives me pause, and I recall another phrase that she once uttered. "Every now and then, the shit magnet flips polarity and repels." Because she said it, it must be true.

45 Things I Can't Say to Your Face, Part V

So Betty and I are in her room, watching a junky movie on the Lifetime channel. Some cheap horror thing about a serial-killing stepfather who gives pretty Penn Badgley the hairy eyeball before trying to whack the sucker. I haven't seen it before (wasn't assigned to it, praise the lawd), and neither have you, I'm betting. You and I caught some stinkers together, but *this*. This is seriously awful.

Just wait, I say to Betty. The villain's gonna pull up in a car just as the heroes are rifling through his bedroom, looking for clues. You'll see.

Sure enough, the villain pulls up in a car just as the heroes are rifling through his bedroom, looking for clues. Betty flicks a look my way.

Ha! There it is, I say. All bad movies are alike! Ever notice that?

Betty just smiles cryptically in reply, turns her attention back to the TV.

What's your favorite movie? I ask.

Again, she smiles cryptically.

What's your favorite movie, Betty? Do you have one?

"When you're here," she says. "You are." So now it's my turn to smile.

But what sort of movie am I? I ask her. Am I a comedy, or am I a tragedy?

This time, just the corner of her mouth ticks up.

"A mystery," she says. And I could not agree more.

I, the jobless Job, surrender to bafflement. To ignorance. To Not Knowing a Darn Thing, Ever. That's my only salvation, in every sense: To give in to the contradictions of everyday life. To resign myself to this state of perpetual cluelessness in the face of concomitant suffering and joy.

And what about you, the once and forever Chris? Jeanne was right: Where you are now, you don't give two shits. You know that nothing matters and everything matters, that all is one and one is all, and both are a holy mess. But what do you care! You're floating around in ecstasy! I am neither floating nor ecstatic, at the moment. Instead, I am earthbound and trapped in the pickle of living. I still give a shit, probably two shits, maybe more.

One night, thumbing through the New Testament, a line from Hebrews grabs my attention: "By faith we understand that the universe was formed at God's command, so that what is seen was not made out of what was visible." Seen comes from the unseen; light comes from the dark. The knowable comes from the un-knowable. Substance comes from absence, creation comes from emptiness, and something comes from its extraterrestrial antecedent: not a Nothing, but a pre-Something, a non-Something, a Soon to Be.

Huh.

Don't theoretical physicists ask the same questions? What formed the universe? What sparked the Big Bang? From what lump of darkness formed the light of septillions of stars? Father Chris had it right: All is paradox. God and love and life are all a mystery, comedy and tragedy both, too much and too awe-ful to comprehend. All we can do is yield to it. All we can know is that we can't. Visible from invisible. Light from dark. Joy from pain, and back again.

I don't get it and never will, I swear. When you first stopped sleeping—and then when you got sick, and then when you got worse, and then when you got hospitalized, and then when you jumped—I tried to find some logic to it. But there wasn't any logic to your death, any more than there was logic to your life and all that you gave me. Was there logic in the way you held first me, then our three babies? In the way your heart thundered in your chest? Why was I blessed with twenty years of marriage to you, extraordinary man? How did we bring such spirited, resilient children into the world? I don't know. I can't know. At times, when I think of you, I'm stabbed with love and anguish all at once. For a moment they're indistinguishable, and I'm confounded.

One Saturday afternoon, Alicia comes over for tea. We remember the vats of Crisis Ziti that landed on the porch after you died — a portent of doom as certain as it is delicious. Anyone who gets handed a tin of that stuff should know they're in trouble. "Do not ask for whom the ziti is baked," Alicia quips. "It's baked for thee!"

I laugh so hard I almost snort tea out my nose.

Maybe laughter is *it*, I say. Maybe laughter is the only bridge we have between the light and the dark, the joy and the pain. . . It's our only way of residing in both at once — in this life, anyway.

Huh.

The next day, sitting outside as Mitchell skateboards with a friend, I consider this again. I recall your laugh, which welled up and seized you and snapped back your head. I think about childbirth, the belly-aching laugh that ends with a baby: agony and ecstasy in one explosive package. I think about the comic, the tragic, the mysterious — and the puzzle of being alive. Each laugh I've laughed this past year has been a tiny blitzkrieg of light, a microcosmic Big Bang that sent forth sparks of joy from the blackness. Is there laughter where you are, my husband? Do you even need it there? Perhaps you don't. Perhaps, in the eternal, paradoxical, unending enchilada where you reside, even the black is brilliant with love. Everything is laughter, all the time.

46 Oh My God

A job. I got one. A good one. Nearby. At the *Times Union*. With health coverage. A miracle. Already. No shit.

The editor calls to tell me the news. I can't believe it. Can. Not. Fuck. Ing. Be. Lieve. It.

This is a man who visited my home on the night of my husband's death, so he knows me. He knows my backstory. I have no problem revealing myself as a hysterical widow, desperate for some change in fortune—and dubious when it arrives.

Is this real? I ask him.

"This is real," he says.

You're not kidding? I ask him.

"I'm not kidding," he says.

Oh my God, I say.

I'm jumping up and down in the kitchen, barely containing my squeals. Jeanne and Mitchell are in the kitchen with me. They throw me bewildered looks that say WHAT IS GOING ON HERE, MOTHER? and I respond by scrawling the word JOB on the back of an envelope.

They know that I mean paid work, not some long-dead compatriot from the Hebrew Bible. So they, too, jump up and down, barely containing their squeals. When I hang up, we stop containing them. Oh my God. Oh my God.

I'm so relieved—not just for me, but for them. Not just because of the paycheck and all that it means (although food is always nice to have around). I'm relieved to show them that Aunt Pam was right; the shit magnet pulled a 180 and repelled.

That the aim of Mitchell's prayer was true; the bad stuff rolled out, and the good stuff rolled in. That fate can do us a favor, once in a while.

Today they see me as a lucky gal. And I am.

When I zap out the news to close friends and family, I'm flooded with love and congratulations. Randy's response makes my day. "Amazing," he writes, "that they would hire such a bitch." And I can just see the quirking of his brow.

47 The Checkout Line Jollies, Part III

It's Saturday morning, and I'm standing in the checkout line with bananas. Lots and lots of bananas. Only later does their symbolic significance hit me with full, phallic force. But for now, there is nothing symbolic about them. They are fruit. I am buying them. Behind me, a voice pipes up.

"Would you trust those?".

A male voice.

Trust what? I wonder. The bananas? Certainly, I'd trust the bananas. They're looking pretty fresh, green just turning to yellow.

But he doesn't mean the bananas. I grasp this when I turn back and glance at the owner of the voice, a rangy, somewhat disarrayed-looking fifty-ish gentleman with a wide smile and uncombed hair. He gestures toward a checkout display of pregnancy tests, selling for the low, low price of $1 a pop. I see his point. Kind of cheap for such a critical product.

Well, look, I say. You could always buy them in bulk. HOLY SHIT, I think. DID I JUST SAY THAT? (*Mouth? Is that you, Mouth?*)

He laughs. He has a big laugh. My Man Radar clicks on.

Not that I'd care, I add. I'm well past that point, anyway. HOLY SHIT. DID I JUST SAY THAT, TOO? Holy shit. I did. I just told a perfect stranger in a grocery checkout line that I am not at present getting laid. Or that I'm past my prime for baby-making. Or quite possibly both.

Holy shit. Holy shit. Holy shit.

"My name's John," he says, extending his hand. "Since I know so much about you already, I figure I should introduce myself."

Amy, I tell him, taking his hand. It's a large hand. He's a large man. He smiles.

The checkout girl, who doesn't look old enough to drive, shoots the both of us a look that says, Jeeeeeesus, are these gray-haired nimrods actually flirting? Then she shoots me a look that says, Get a grip and swipe your bank card, lady. I try, but I screw up. She tells me to swipe it again. I try, but I screw up.

The third time I try and screw up, I turn to the Concerned Pharmaceutical Consumer behind me and say, This is obviously a ruse. I'm obviously trying to prolong this conversation as much as possible.

"Obviously," he says, smiling again. Then: "Ecuador?"

He's spotted my purse, a colorful little number Madeleine gave me for Christmas. The name of the country of origin is emblazoned across the side. I say, Why yes, Ecuador. My oldest spent a gap year there.

"No kidding!"

No kidding. She's a great kid. Starting Georgetown, I say. And then: You have kids?

He has kids. Two. One is 23 and making her way, one is 17 and unsure about college. As he tells me about them, the cashier rings up his groceries, and I pack up my bananas into bags—it's one of those bag-your-own discount joints—as slowly as possible. My Man Radar is now going ballistic. I was never any good at flirting, I've never figured out the arcane shit of the supermarket come-on, and I wonder what I ought to do next. Bat my eyelashes? Ask for his phone number? Sack him and slam him to the ground? He's ringless, but God knows what that means. F.S.O. is a murky and inexact science when it comes to the *digitus anularis* of male left hand. This is the sort of thing I didn't give a damn about when I was married; what did I care if a man was single, or married, or dating, or gay, or asexual, or a priest? What did I care about the art of seduction?

He bags up his stuff and we mosey into the parking lot.

Nice chatting with you, I say. And then: I bet you use that pregnancy-test line on all the girls.

(Holy shit!)

"Oh, yes. I'll have to try it again sometime. It worked so well."

(Holy shit! Holy shit!)

Pretty sly operator, I say. Well, I hope to bump into you in the check-out line again sometime. Giggle.

(Hooooooly SHIT!)

"I look forward to it," he says.

And so we split for our separate cars. I briefly consider stalking him—maybe I should just track him back to his house and boil his rabbit! Bwahahahahah!—before my super-ego pimp-slaps my id, and not a moment too soon.

I fire up the engine, overjoyed to be a breathing, functioning female who, against all odds, still merits masculine attention. Who knew? Another milestone in my grief: For the first time in decades, I've flirted with a stranger. He's flirted with me.

Holy shit.

I drive home with my phallic bananas.

48 Belaying and Belayed

One of Mitchell's buddies, a terrific kid with a terrific mohawk, dangles in the air six feet above me. This was not part of the plan. The plan was for him to ascend the wall at this indoor climbing gym, then descend, then unhook the carabiner attaching him to the rope and the rope to my carabiner to me, and then run off and join the rest of the kids now spelunking through a labyrinthine network of artificial caves. But Matty is adventurous. Matty wanted to try climbing first. So Matty attached himself to me, an umbilical roped between us, and quickly clambered up a high wall dotted with colorful hand- and toeholds. Halfway up, his foot slipped. He lost his balance, flailed at a handhold and bounced away and off the wall, falling in a dead drop until the belay device anchored at my midriff did its appointed job.

And so he swings and twirls above my head, his weight yanking at my belly.

Matty, I bleat. Matty, don't worry, Matty, I'll get you down.

"OK," he says.

I'll lower you now, all right?

"OK," he says again, and I must say, this boy is being preternaturally calm about the whole thing. That, or he's putting on a brave face while quietly spazzing, just as I am quietly spazzing at the thought of someone else's child relying on me so literally for support. We send our babies into the cold hard world on faith that some warm, soft, benevolent piece of it will catch them if they fall, and we like to think we'd do the same for other people's babies. But I tend to interpret both the "falling" and "catching" bits as figurative.

Here I am. I caught this kid. Nothing figurative about it. Holy mackerel.

Once down and earthbound, and released from his carabiner, Matty scoots off to the caves with the rest of Mitchell's tribe, and I hook myself up to Jane. We take turns belaying and climbing, catching and falling, heading up these rough plastic palisades with nothing but a cord and our trust (in anchors, in pulleys, in one another) to hold us. I fall and fall again, knocking my face and then my leg against the wall. Blood wells up on my kneecap. I sweat like a pig. Once, midway up, my left leg cramps, but I stretch it and keep going, damned if I'll let my body or my fear prevent me from reaching the top.

I'm new to climbing, and I love how it feels. "Climbing is seventy percent legs, thirty percent arms," says the young man in charge, a hoarse, skinny lad who shouts out instructions so artfully strange that they ought to get funding from the NEA. But he's right about the arms and legs: Push, don't pull. Press, don't haul. With my low center of gravity, I like the reliance on my bottommost limbs, and I like the sense of exhausted accomplishment when I make it all the way up and back. I like everything about this: how difficult it is, how technical it is, how much thought it takes and balance it requires. Any activity that makes a grieving widow feel strong and self-reliant is a powerfully addictive and sexy, sexy thing. I need more of this, I decide. I crave it. I demand it. I am the Wasted Widow. Hear me roar.

Lately I've started to regard my aloneness and manlypantslessness as somehow pathological. Not the being-alone part. I mean the fixating-on-being-alone part. Having been foisted into this new, solitary existence against my will, I've fought against it tooth and nail. From the get-go it felt like an abomination. Even at first, when I could not have conceived of welcoming another man into my life and my heart, the barbaric deprivation of it pained me.

Then the switch flipped, and I wanted another man, and I yearned for a White Knight in sparkling armor to gallop up with his muscular arms and bad handwriting and sweep me away. Or if he couldn't sweep me away, maybe he could give me a backrub. Or hug me some night while I sob until I retch; that'd be swell. At its most insane, this urge for a man dwelt on the paradoxical return of my dead husband, as in: CHRIS should be holding me! CHRIS should be comforting me! CHRIS should be here helping me through THE WORST FUCKING CRISIS OF MY LIFE, forgetting for a spell that his death actually prompted said fucking crisis.

But now I've passed a rough year since he died—rough in so many ways—and I can see how far I've climbed. I look back on all those long and lonely and effluvia-filled nights, and I think, Hot damn, girlfriend! You did that yourself! Without any assistance from a Manly Pants! And I feel a budding retroactive pride, as though I've just received a Nobel prize for all those hours alone in the lab, cold pizza beside me, with only a three-legged rat and a petri dish for company.

So often I've heard myself characterized as "strong." But I've never felt it. Not till now. Not until I glance down at all the days below me, and I understand that I climbed them myself.

49 Isabella

One morning, I drop off the car at the mechanic's and hoof back home through some muggy gray stuff passing for air. I pass my neighbor, Isabella, on her stoop, watering impatiens. She is ninety-two and radiant in bright magenta pants.

Good morning, Isabella! Great color on you!

She turns.

How are you? I ask.

"Fine, fine. I thought I would water these. I don't know why," she says, gesturing to the flowers. They look a little sad: wilting, browning, on their way out. She considers them. Sprinkles more water on them. Turns again, slowly.

"But they looked thirsty," she says. "So I'm watering them. Even though they're dying." Then she throws me a grin. "And so am I."

But who isn't? I say, and we both laugh.

Really, who isn't?

I live two houses down on this modest and generous block. It's a dead end in every good sense: a place where people come, raise kids, stay put, get old and die. In the 19 years since Chris and I first moved in, a small mob of babies, ours among them, had spilled out onto the street and morphed into toddlers, then school kids, then teens, all while the empty-nesters turned silver and happy with grandchildren. And then those grandchildren grew, and the empty-nesters became the old folks who chatted and kept their eye on the street, making meatballs for the block parties and cupcakes for the latest batch of children. Chris and I had said goodbye to some of those old folks. We had been to some of their funerals. I always knew there would be more goodbyes on this dead end, and sooner rather than later; that's how it works around here, how it's supposed to work everywhere. Births and deaths in equal measure. But his death? *His*? How out of whack it seems. Yet death is always out of whack, although I'm not sure why. Everyone knows it's coming. It's not like it never happens. Dying is all natural, so it must be good for us—the organic quinoa of life stages. Then again, even Jesus wept at the news of Lazarus's death. Jesus! The guy with the power to reanimate corpses! He of all people knew he'd be raising his dead friend in just a mo, and still. He cried. So maybe dying is natural, but maybe the weeping is, too.

Isabella, I've decided, has the right approach. Given that everyone is fading like impatiens in the low September sun, we should all bend our faces toward the daylight. We should wear the purple pants. Water the flowers on the stoop. Look up and greet our neighbors. Live.

50 Snails

Months after Hayden unleashed the Wasted Widow, it's Tamar's turn to ply me with liquor. I'm at her house in Cambridge for a party, and she offers me wine.

I know you want to get me drunk, I tell her. But I'm hittin' the seltzer first. It's 5:30, I haven't eaten anything since pulling out of my driveway three and a half hours earlier, and I don't want to start bumping into tables until at least 7 o'clock.

Go, New Amy.

The house, a warm, broad colonial that Tamar shares with her husband, Louis, is quickly filling up with friends from their Harvard years. It's their 30th reunion—what would have been my sister Lucy's 30th reunion—and they're hosting a Friday-night warm-up in their home. Most of these folks I first met when I was fifteen and took the train to Boston to visit my brainiac big sister. Some I've kept in touch with through the years: Tamar, Louis, Sue, Tony. Some I remember, but haven't seen in decades. Others I don't recall in the slightest: Either I forgot them after brief inconsequential meetings over potato puffs in the Adams House dining hall, or I never met them at all.

One is standing in the kitchen with a couple of friends. Don't think I know the guy. Don't think I ever met him, over tater tots or anything else.

Hi, I say, proffering a hand. I'm Amy. Lucy's kid sister.

His face lights up. He has smiling eyes. A gentle manner. Handsome.

"Joe," he says.

Joe.

I furtively check out his left hand. Ringless. Hmmm.

We chat about Georgetown, where his oldest just graduated. He tells a hilarious story about her freshman roommate from hell, and he laughs. I laugh. My Man Radar begins to ping; could it be that he's available and might even find me attractive? I check his ring finger again, just to be sure I'm not hallucinating. All clear. The Man Radar pings a little more insistently. After a few minutes we separate and circulate, and I saunter toward Tamar.

I was just talking to Joe, I say. He's *really nice*.

"Joe? Yeah, Joe is a SWEETHEART," she ventures, and before I can ask it, she answers my question. "He's here with his girlfriend."

Drat. He's here with his girlfriend. I make a mental note to take my Man Radar in for a tune-up, because it is obviously malfunctioning. Then I move to another part of the kitchen and engage in another conversation with another clutch of Harvard friends. Joe melts into the group from the opposite end of the room, and once more we wind up talking.

Again, my Man Radar begins to ping. It's a distraction, and I wish it would shut the hell up. Curse you, defective Man Radar! You are giving me false hopes! But we talk some more, and we laugh some more, and he smiles some more from his mouth to his warm brown eyes, and all the while I'm receiving a loud, high-pitched whine that's inaudible to everyone else but threatens to make my head explode. I think: If only this sweet, smiling Joe-Being were unattached, I would commence flirting with him in earnest. But he isn't, so I console myself by simply enjoying his company. There is much to enjoy.

Sometime after midnight, the party breaks up with promises to reconvene soon. Joe hugs me on the way out.

I think: A hug? That was a pleasant surprise. What did it mean? Assuming it meant anything. Did it mean something?

I'm staying over, so I hang back with Tamar and Louis as they send their classmates into the autumn night. Once they've all bustled out the door, I resume my inquisition of Tamar.

Joe...? I begin.

"Yes? Joe?"

Joe...and his girlfriend. How long have they been together?

"Oh, that wasn't his girlfriend after all. I was wrong. She was just a friend. He gave her a ride to the party."

I say to myself:

SQUEEEEEEEEEEEEEEEEEEEEEEEEEEEEEEEEEEEEEEEEEE, he's single! He's single! He's single!

I say to Tamar:

He's, umm, really nice. And, umm, really cute.

"Yes, he is."

And then I say it again:

He's *really* nice. And *really* cute. Is he seeing someone else?

Tamar isn't sure, but she promises to investigate over the weekend. And again I say to myself: SQUEEEEEEEEEEEEEEEE!

When her inquiry turns up insufficient information, I make a bold and decisive move. I ask her for Joe's email address, and I zap him a message cold. He responds right away. He tells me he's glad I came to the party. And we begin emailing each other daily, sometimes twice daily, sometimes more. Then we decide to meet for lunch midway between Albany, where I am, and New Jersey, where he is. He chooses a French restaurant with solid Yelp ratings. We agree to meet at noon on a Wednesday.

The day arrives. I am, as I was in the foaming Ecuadorian whitewater, scared shitless. But I plan to ride this wave. I won't get tossed.

My dad calls the morning of. Asks me what I'm planning to wear. I go into a small fit of anxiety trying to answer.

A nice top, I finally squeak out. And nice jeans. And nice earrings.

"Which earrings?"

Did you just ask that for real, or are you giving me grief?

"I'm giving you grief."

Somehow, I manage to drive downstate without crashing. Somehow, I manage to parallel park the car without denting bumpers in front and behind. Somehow, I manage to walk without tripping to the restaurant and plant myself outside at the appointed hour. Somehow, I manage to not faint when Joe walks up, resplendent in a blue blazer and crisp striped shirt.

My heart leaps. Good lord, he's attractive.

Once inside, we order squash soup, and snails, and duck, and talk about our drives from south and north. When the snails arrive, Joe shows me how to eat them: dipped in plenty of butter. He lived in France for a while and knows his way around gastropods. They're new to me. I try one.

Oh my God, I say. It's delicious.

Joe smiles—again with the eyes, always the eyes—and lowers another snail into the sea of butter. I watch him, and I'm astonished. Astonished that I can do this. Astonished that I can go on a date. Astonished that I can feel anything, anything at all, after the death and devastation that came before. Astonished that I don't feel guilty. Astonished to believe, instead, that Chris is happy for me. Astonished to find myself in the low light of a French restaurant, eating snails with a handsome man.

~ Chris Ringwald ~

In his 55 years of living, Christopher D. Ringwald crammed it in. A Bronx native who carried the pluck of that great borough wherever he went, he worked as a carpenter, construction contractor, human rights lobbyist and lay missionary in Peru— teaching carpentry to mountain villagers—before making the switch to journalism.

He did not waste a word or a moment in his writing, his reporting, his life, and he devoted himself always to understanding and clarifying the plight of those less fortunate than he: the addicted, the poor, the innocents struck by crossfire. In 1999, he traveled to Iraq to report on the effects of the sanctions on civilians; in 2005 he traveled to northern Uganda to report on the effects of the conflict on children. For the Albany *Times Union*, where he spent several years on several beats, he wrote a series of articles that inspired a new state law establishing performance standards for substance-abuse programs. His commentary, on matters social and religious, appeared in *The Wall Street Journal, The New York Times, The Washington Post*, and other prominent publications, but he brought the same rigorous logic and prevailing warmth to the smallest conversations with friends.

He wrote three books: *A Day Apart: How Jews, Christians, and Muslims Find Faith, Freedom, and Joy on the Sabbath* (Oxford, 2008); *The Soul of Recovery: Uncovering the Spiritual Dimension in the Treatment of Addictions* (Oxford, 2002); and *Faith in Words: Ten Writers Reflect on the Spirituality of Their Profession* (ACTA, 1997). A graduate of Georgetown University, he earned a master's in journalism from Columbia and a master's in theology from St. Bernard's Institute. He spent three years editing *The Evangelist*, a regional Catholic weekly based in Albany.

Intellectual curiosity, old-world chivalry and bedrock decency marked his days. He was a devout Catholic and a moral man. He loved family, friends, humanity, and God, and he loved to think, talk, teach, read, write, laugh, play, pray, grapple with big issues, help others, and challenge all who knew him to be more honest and giving. He made the world a better place, and it misses him.

Acknowledgments

Four remarkable women featured in this book have died since I first wrote it: my second mother, Pat Richardson, whose love, insight and calm acceptance graced my life for 36 years; my best friend, the humble and hilarious Pam Bond Nicholson, who helped me through my writing as she helped me through my grief; and my friends Betty Ryan and Isabelle Carey (whom Chris always called "Isabella"), both of them longtime sources of wry observation and wisdom.

Who *wasn't* walking beside me that first year, nudging me forward, giving me strength? They are almost too many to mention.

Thanks and love go first to my three beautiful, spirited and inspiring children, Madeleine, Jeanne and Mitchell Ringwald, whose presence on this earth and in my life fills me with gratitude and wonder. The same goes for my splendiferous second father, Dan Richardson, and the whole amazing clan: Betsy Richardson; Randy, Susi, Liza, and Josh Richardson; Danny Richardson and Denise Vaillancourt, and Tanner, Cooper, and Walker Richardson; Connie and Avery Royster; and Nils Haaland and Sherri Geerdes. They let me know, loudly and often, that I and my children would never be alone.

Thanks and love, too, to Chris's spectacularly kind and supportive family: Marie Ringwald and Michael Kerr, Carl Ringwald and Karin Thurmon, Anne and Bobby D'Adamo, Tom and Paula Ringwald; and Mike Ringwald, Steve Ringwald and Jen Chappell, and Chris Ringwald and Emma Cooke. They reached for us, held onto us and never let us go.

Next, Bob. This volume would not exist at all were it not for the inspiration and constant, gentle nagging of my dear friend Robert Whitaker, whose heart is even bigger than his laugh. The stories began with an email to him and exploded when I phoned him with the tale of the Hitchhiker—and, hearing him dissolve in laughter, joked that "I ought to write a book." Bob decided I wasn't joking and thereafter wouldn't leave me alone. He read the manuscript at various stages, offered sage advice and connected me with his agent, the awesome Jane Dystel. Thank you, Bob. Thank you, Jane. And thanks to Miriam Goderich and all at Dystel & Goderich Literary Management.

Thanks also to my zesty, perspicacious, and creative editor, Lynn Price, and everyone at Behler Publications, who took a wild leap of faith when they agreed to publish my unhinged little memoir. They took another wild leap when my daughter Madeleine, in a stroke of genius, suggested putting a plunger on the cover.

Thanks to Jane Gottlieb and her son, Maxim, for eating with us, being with us, being family to us, being part of our lives and the book. Thanks to others who read the manuscript and bucked up my spirits at critical junctures: Bill Dentzer, Tamar Zimmerman, Celina Ottaway, Donald Munro, Toni Bosco, Susan Friend Fisher, Winnie Yu, Dan Mandel, Bill and Rebecca Boardman, Cameron McWhirter, and Alicia and Joe Stenard.

Speaking of Joe, thanks to my buddies and bandmates in the Maraca Incident: Dennis Gaffney and Kathy Ray, Chris and Carolyn Boldiston, Kristin Barron and Steve Shashok, James Peltz and Ruth Ann Smalley, Aviva Bower and Mark Wolfe, Alexa Bontempo and Brian Borton. And thanks to my countless other friends and neighbors in the Grove Avenue Gang and the Helderberg auxiliary.

Thanks to Allie and Charlotte Mitchell, Karen and Travis Nelson and all the Mitchells; to Margaret, Murray, and all the Weissbachs; to Biancollis one and all; to Sue Cheng, for being such an important part of the year's first week and the book's first chapter; to Joe Profaci, for being such an important part of the last. Thanks also to the various and sundry characters, named and unnamed, whose stories intersected with mine and landed in my book.

For their compassion and spiritual guidance, I'm grateful to Father Bob Longobucco and Father Chris DeGiovine; to Betsy Rowe-Manning and the St. Vincent de Paul parish, especially its choir and band; to Diana Conroy and Fred Boehrer of Emmaus House, the Albany Catholic Worker House; and to Jo Massarelli and Marc Tumeinski of the Catholic Worker community in Worcester.

Further thanks to Chris's many and supportive friends; to all of our newspaper colleagues who reached out; to the Times Union, for permission to excerpt my old Clooney review; to the magnificent offspring of everyone mentioned above; and to all of my children's friends, coaches and teachers who were present in so many ways.

Finally: My deepest gratitude goes out to everyone not yet thanked who dropped a plate of ziti or yummy something on our porch—or shared a kind word, a hug, a thought, a laugh, a lift, a gift, a tune, a prayer, a squeeze of the hand or a quiet, unsung favor. Together you showed me that community is a webbing made with love. I could not have lived through this, or written about it, without you.